TABLE OF CONTENTS

ILLUSTRATIONS ii

INTRODUCTION 1

    Background 4
    Thesis 5
    Methodology 6

THE HISTORY OF LARGE CITIES 8

CLASSIFYING LARGE CITIES 10

OPERATIONAL FRAMEWORKS AND CASE STUDIES: 1944-1969 13

    FM 31-50, 1944 14
    Manila, 1944 15
    Berlin and Tokyo, 1945 17
    Korea, 1950... 23
    FM 31-50, 1952 and FM 31-50, 1964 27
    Saigon, 1968 31

OPERATIONAL FRAMEWORK: 1977-2001 37

    FM 90-10, 1977 39
    FM 90-10, 1979 42

CONCLUSIONS 44

    Panama City, 1989 44
    Trends 49
    Recent U.S. Army, Joint, and Departmental Efforts............. 51
    Implications.. 56

BIBLIOGRAPHY 60

i

ILLUSTRATIONS

Page

Figure 1. São Paulo. 12

Figure 2. Berlin's military to civil transition. 19

Figure 3. Attack from above. 27

Figure 4. Attack through ceiling and wall. 30

Figure 5. The German Democratic Republic and the Federal Republic of Germany. 39

Figure 6. Building patterns. 43

Figure 7: Pathologies and ecologies. 55

"I have neither desires nor fears," the Khan declared, "and my dreams are composed either by my mind or by chance."

"Cities also believe they are the work of the mind or of chance, but neither the one nor the other suffices to hold up their walls. You take delight not in a city's seven or seventy wonders, but in the answer it gives to a question of yours."

"Or the question it asks you, forcing you to answer, like Thebes through the mouth of the Sphinx."

—Kublai Khan and Marco Polo, as imagined by Italo Calvino in *Invisible Cities*

INTRODUCTION

A remarkable number of military studies of cities published over the past forty years begin with the following quote from Sun Tzu, as translated by Samuel Griffith in 1971: "Attack cities only when there is no alternative."[1] Roger Ames, translating Sun Tzu over two decades later, interprets the same passage as, ". . . resort to assaulting walled cities only when there is no other choice."[2]

The difference in translation – the specifying of *walled* cities as those that the general should avoid attacking – may seem a minor one. On the contrary – to the military professional charged with operating in a large city, this represents a significant difference in interpretation with important ramifications for urban operations. Ames' translation, which is based both on deeper cultural appreciation and large passages of the original Sun Tzu discovered in archaeological digs long after Griffith's efforts, reveals that Sun Tzu recognized differences in urban environments, particularly those that warrant increased protection. As early as the Warring States period in ancient China, cities began to vary in manner of construction and organization, based largely on their size and political importance. These factors led directly to increasing levels

---

[1] Sun Tzu, *The Art of War*, trans., Samuel B. Griffith (London, UK: Oxford Univ. Press, 1971), 78.

[2] Sun Tzu, *The Art of War: The First English Translation Incorporating the Recently Discovered Yin-Ch'üeh-Shan Texts*, trans., Roger T. Ames (New York, NY: Ballantine Books, 1993), 111.

of defensive protection around the largest and most important cities, including walls and other methods of protection against siege and assault, which required an attacker to use more time-consuming and costly methods when attacking particularly large cities.[3]

This differentiation between cities based on their size and defensibility remains absent from current U.S. Army doctrine. Further, the taxonomy of large cities appears on only one page in doctrine written since 1944. This is not only a doctrinal issue, however. When he wrote *The Art of War,* Sun Tzu did not allude to military fortifications in isolation. He was intimating that cities with walls possessed an advantage in their ability to withstand attack, which often resulted in their development into major centers of commerce and culture.[4] Therefore, when cities grow to a certain size, they take on unique properties. These properties remain uninvestigated, at least in U.S. Army doctrinal publications. Further compounding the matter, no guidance exists in either U.S. joint doctrine or departmental policy regarding operations in large cities. Such operations pose unique challenges not only to the force, but also to the operational planners who lay the foundations for military success or failure when describing and directing orders to that force.[5]

Different urban environments possess many varying attributes. Although cities have emerged and developed in different parts of the world over the past 10,000 years, one can detect a surprising degree of order and similarity when arranging facts about them.[6] For example, cities share several common physical qualities. Most cities exist in close proximity to water and good

[3]Sun Tzu, *The Art of War*, trans., Ralph D. Sawyer (Boulder, CO: Westview Press, 1994), 177.

[4]Lewis Mumford, *The City in History: Its Origins, Its Transformations, and Its Prospects*, 1st ed. (New York, NY: Harcourt, 1961), 250.

[5]Department of the Army, Army Doctrine and Training Publiciation (ADP) 5-0, *The Operations Process*, (Washington, DC: Headquarters, Department of the Army, 2012), 9-10.

[6]Ian Morris, "Social Development", Stanford, CA, http://www.ianmorris.org (course materials accessed March 2012); Eliyahu M. Goldratt and Jeff Cox, *The Goal: A Process of Ongoing Improvement*, Kindle ed. (Great Barrington, MA: North River Press, 2004), 4740-4747.

soil; remain accessible to occupants yet easily defended from enemies; and need to be near sources of fish or shellfish in order to thrive.[7] On the other hand, cities possess important intangible qualities as well. These myriad cultural and other informal social structures defy graphic or narrative representation, leading to difficulty establishing causal links to explain the dynamic nature of the environment and populations of different cities.[8] All cities are unique and while one may perceive commonality and pattern, these perception-dependent representations reflect only varying degrees of accuracy.[9] Thus, information about a particular city will always be an incomplete or distorted description of its actual characteristics that says as much about the observer as the observed city.[10]

According to theorist John Boyd, the practice of warfare involves imposing order over chaos to provide predictability to the strategist or policymaker.[11] Yet, neither the U.S. Army nor any department of the U.S. Government has provided guidelines to the force for operations in large cities. The frequency with which those strategists and policymakers rely on the U.S. Army to conduct operations in large cities highlights the importance of understanding their ever-changing characteristics. In fact, multiple independent congressional studies suggest that the military, and in particular, the U.S. Army, will always have responsibility for public order, security, and emergency services during and after conflicts or disasters; the Department of

---

[7]Mumford, 17.

[8]Everett C. Dolman, *Pure Strategy: Power and Principle in the Space and Information Age* (New York, NY: Frank Cass), 13.

[9]Jonah Lehrer, *How We Decide* (Boston, MA: Houghton Mifflin Harcourt, 2009), 65.

[10]Alan Beyerchen, "Clausewitz, Nonlinearity, and the Unpredictability of War," *International Security* 17, no. 3 (1992): 77.

[11]Frans P. B. Osinga, *Science, Strategy and War: The Strategic Theory of John Boyd* (New York, NY: Routledge, 2007), 10.

Defense confirms this responsibility in its capstone authorities document.[12] These activities will not always require improving the conditions beyond the status quo. Not every endeavor must aim to transform large cities into something beyond their reach; not every operation must echo Augustus' hollow epitaph: "I found Rome of clay; I leave it to you of marble."[13] Nevertheless, the U.S. Army operates in large cities relatively often, and when it does, it must conduct combat and stability operations to provide security and enable governance both in tandem and in an integral manner.[14]

Background

Since 1944, the U.S. Army has operated in nine foreign cities with populations of more than 750,000 people (metropolises). These operations have ranged from foreign humanitarian assistance to amphibious assaults. In some cases, such as in Manila, U.S. Army organizations have adapted well to these unique environs. In others, such as Saigon, they have failed to exploit opportunities or consolidate hard-won gains. While U.S. Army doctrine addresses urban environments, it focuses merely on tactical action.[15]

---

[12]David P. Auerswald and Colton C. Campbell, *Congress and the Politics of National Security* (New York, NY: Cambridge University Press, 2012), 65-68; Samuel R. Berger et al., *In the Wake of War: Improving U.S. Post-Conflict Capabilities; Report of an Independent Task Force Sponsored by the Council on Foreign Relations*, Independent Task Force Report (New York: Council on Foreign Relations, 2005), 13. Campbell, 65-68; Department of Defense, Department of Defense Directive (DoDD) 5100.01, *Functions of the Department of Defense and Its Major Components*, (Washington, DC: The Department of Defense, 2010), 29.

[13]Cassius Dio, *Roman History, Volume VII, Books 56-60*, ed. G.P. Goold, trans., Cary. Earnest, Loeb Classical Library, vol. VII (Suffolk, UK: St. Edmundsbudy Press, 2000), 69.

[14]Nadia Schadlow, "War and the Art of Governance," *Parameters: Journal of the US Army War College* 33, (2003): 86.

[15]Department of the Army, Field Manual (FM) 3-06, *Urban Operations*, (Washington, DC: Headquarters, Department of the Army, 2006),

That is not the only oversight, however, as the body of doctrine does not address large cities – those that have a population over 750,000. Large cities take on special properties in both the social force required to maintain them and the manner in which urban experts recognize and label them because of the complexity of their inherent systems.[16] This social force manifests in terms of cultural and developmental factors that challenge both cognitive externalization tools and traditional cartography. Further, no U.S. Army framework exists for assessing or planning in large cities. Even at the joint or departmental level, U.S. Army personnel can find no helpful references in dealing with operations in large cities. While many emerging constructs have recently appeared in U.S. Army and joint discourse that incorporate a bevy of novel military theories, no current document addresses large cities specifically or directly.[17] Given the ever-increasing number and significance of large cities across the world, the U.S. Army will almost certainly continue to operate in these unique environs. Therefore, Army doctrine writers must determine, and incorporate into urban operations manuals, what special considerations the U.S. Army must take into account when preparing or conducting operations in large cities.

Thesis

All cities are unique – large cities are especially so. Existing frameworks to classify and understand metropolises for the purposes of practicing both operational planning and operational art fail to account for many factors of significance to both the operating force and the city's

---

[16]UN Department of Economic and Social Affairs Population Division, "Population of Urban Agglomerations with 750,000 Inhabitants or More in 2011, by Country, 1950-2025 (Thousands)," in *Excel*, WUP2011-F12-Cities_Over_750K.xls (New York, NY: United Nations, 2011).

[17]Department of the Army, Field Manual (FM) 2-91.4, *Intelligence Support to Urban Operations*, (Washington, DC: Headquarters, Department of the Army, 2008), 1-2 and 1-3; The Joint Staff, Joint Publication (JP) 3-06, *Joint Urban Operations*, (Washington, DC: Headquarters, The Joint Staff, 2009), I-1.

inhabitants. Until the U.S. Army publishes doctrine for operating in large cities, it will continue to face challenges exploiting opportunities or consolidating gains in this complex and unique terrain.

Methodology

To understand the unique nature of large cities, one must situate them within the range of human population densities, from the largely rural existence of human society for most of its history, to the relatively new urbanization of the past few centuries. With the phenomenon of urbanization explained, one can turn to investigations into the history of cities that reveal common accepted practices for classifying all urban development, and in particular, for identifying particular cities as "large," or "metropolises." These investigations show that since the rise of urbanization, those cities that have reached a population of over 750,000 inhabitants tend to exhibit the characteristics of a metropolis. Further, studies of metropolises enable identification and analysis of the unique characteristics of these large cities that set them apart from smaller urban areas.[18]

With the urbanization of much of the modern world explained, and the characteristics of large cities identified and contrasted with those of smaller cities, one can begin to apply these ideas in the evaluation of military campaigns in the metropolis. Given space constraints, this study cannot include all U.S. Army operations in large cities; therefore, the following analysis includes only such operations that have taken place from 1944 to 2001. Despite this delimitation,

---

[18]Mumford, 75; Lewis Mumford, *The Culture of Cities* (New York, NY: Harcourt, 1938), 65; UN Department of Economic and Social Affairs Population Division, WUP2011-F12-Cities_Over_750K.xls; World Bank, *Reshaping Economic Geography*, World Development Report (Washington, DC: World Bank, 2009), 6; Demographia, "Demographia World Urban Areas" http://www.demographia.com/db-worldua.pdf (2012); Dolores Hayden, *Building Suburbia: Green Fields and Urban Growth, 1820-2000* (New York, NY: Pantheon Books, 2003), 10; Joanne P. Sharp, *Geographies of Postcolonialism: Spaces of Power and Representation* (Los Angeles, CA: SAGE, 2009), 24.

many relevant and varied cases exist, including operations in Manila, Berlin, Tokyo, Seoul, Saigon, and Panama City.

Comparative analyses of these historical cases reveals much about the challenges the U.S. Army has typically faced when operating in a metropolis.[19] Future study would find Mogadishu deserving of special mention – although the city at the time only had 350,000-500,000 inhabitants.[20] Additionally, U.S. Army operations in Kabul, Baghdad, and Port au Prince (which swelled to the size of a large city just prior to the 2010 earthquake) are certainly worthwhile, but they have occurred too recently to explore in historical context.[21] In light of these challenges, this study will conclude with a synthesis of trends from U.S. Army operations in large cities prior to the Global War on Terror and the U.S. Army's doctrinal support to this effort. This will highlight the need for a major revision of the U.S. Army's approach to urban operations in large cities. One possible route, described in the section entitled "Implications," draws on two emerging approaches to urban theory.

---

[19]Seperately, domestic operations also warrant further consideration.

[20]Anthony C. Funkhouser, "An Assessment of the IPB Process at the Operational Level" (U.S. Army Command and General Staff College, 1999), 31-32; Art Eggleton, *Report of the Somalia Comission of Inquiry* 1997. Vol. 1, 131. International governments estimated Mogadishu's population in 1993 at 350,000-500,000, depending on the count of refugees in proximity to the city.

[21]Haitian Institute of Statistics and Information, "The Republic of Haiti Administrative Units," in *HTML table*, http://www.ihsi.ht/. (Port Au Prince, Haiti: Ministry of Economy and Finance, 2009). Port au Prince had approximately 704,000 inhabitants in 2003. Classification of information is another challenge concerning all operations in support of the Global War On Terror.

THE HISTORY OF LARGE CITIES

There are myriad explanations and theories for how cities came about. Most of them are realist interpretations ranging from collective security to the invention of metal cisterns.[22] There are undercurrents, however, about the human need for continuity and sense making. As the famous poet Ralph Waldo Emerson quipped, "Our civilization and these ideas are reducing earth to a brain. See how by telegraph and steam…the earth is anthropized," meaning that cities are merely a reflection of humanity's internal processes.[23] To this end, the barbarous, insecure life of the open country without settlement makes a tidy narrative of the history of man, but the reality is much deeper.[24] Cites reflect a need for a meaningful life and continuity with each generation, one that entertains past and future.[25] Once they grew to a certain size, cities began to tie core political areas to surrounding territories, amplifying both the city's size and influence.[26]

These factors have a synergistic effect, and contrary to Plato's description of the ideal city as one limited to the number of citizens that he could address in one sitting, cities continue to grow in both size and number.[27] The first large city, Rome, reached approximately one million occupants during the first century AD.[28] Chang'an, in Central China, reached a population of one

---

[22]Mark E. Eberhart, *Why Things Break: Understanding the World by the Way It Comes Apart*, 1st ed. (New York, NY: Harmony Books, 2003), 21.

[23]Ralph Waldo Emerson, Waldo Emerson Forbes, and Edward Waldo Emerson, *Journals of Ralph Waldo Emerson, with Annotations* (Boston, MA: Houghton Mifflin, 1909), 574.

[24]Mumford, *The Culture of Cities*, 65.

[25]Mumford, *The City in History: Its Origins, Its Transformations, and Its Prospects*, 9.

[26]Jeffrey Ira Herbst, *States and Power in Africa: Comparative Lessons in Authority and Control*, Princeton Studies in International History and Politics (Princeton, NJ: Princeton University Press, 2000), 14.

[27]Plato and David Allan Bloom, *The Republic* (New York, NY: Basic Books, 1968), 49; Mumford, *The City in History: Its Origins, Its Transformations, and Its Prospects*, 63.

[28]Morris, 110.

million around 700 AD. [29] Since then, humans have gradually left behind the hunter-gatherer lifestyle and massed in urban centers, siting and developing ever-larger cities. In 1900, one of every ten people lived in a city – approximately eighteen million people in total.[30] Between 2010 and 2030, more than half of the world's seven billion people will live in cities of some type.[31] According to some estimates, seventy-five percent of the world's nine billion people will live in a city by 2050.[32] This change will eventually lead to current cites becoming megalopolises, or corridors of cities rather than individual municipalities, a phenomenon already taking place in the United States, in regions like Norfolk to Boston, Pittsburg to Chicago, and San Diego to San Francisco.[33]

Regardless of how big they get, now or eventually, large cities have special properties: as they reach a "metropolitan" stage, they require an enormous amount of social force to keep them from collapsing.[34] Classifying this social force is not easy. Not only is it complex, but also challenging at the individual level, to both worldviews and morays. Nevertheless, it is a worthy enterprise on sheer scale alone. In 2010, there were over 646 cities whose population was greater than 750,000.[35] Using simple arithmetic, if about one-half of the world's population lives in

[29]Morris, 118.

[30]Stephen Graham, *Cities Under Siege: The New Military Urbanism* (London, UK: Verso, 2010), 1.

[31]Programme United Nations Human Settlements, *State of the World's Cities 2010/2011: Bridging the Urban Divide* (Washington, DC: Earthscan, 2010), 4.

[32]Graham, 2, 47.

[33]United Nations Human Settlements, 20. This is also called "conurbation." Merriam-Webster defines this term as an aggregation or continuous network of urban communities. Merriam-Webster Inc., *Merriam-Webster's Collegiate Dictionary* (Springfield, MA: Merriam-Webster, 2009).

[34]Mumford, *The Culture of Cities*, 295.

[35]UN Department of Economic and Social Affairs Population Division, WUP2011-F12-

cities, one-half of that population lives in large cities. Put another way, one quarter of the world lives in a large city, and the number is steadily growing.

CLASSIFYING LARGE CITIES

Among the many possible ways to classify a city, one can measure its size and density; however, cities are too complex to define in such simple terms because different bodies define human settlements in different ways. This often stems from political motivations, as ambiguity can be of great help in either garnering or avoiding contributions to national, state, or city level funding.[36] The phenomenon of cities that seem increasingly edgeless, and in some cases endless, further compounds the problem of classification.[37] Once an urban core diffuses from its center, either by manmade or natural delineation, suburbs and exurbs crop up around them.[38] These fringe developments are increasingly common and have special properties of their own. Delores Hayden, a world leader in identifying and classifying sprawl, or unorganized growth from an urban core, notes that while architects design or at least influence most metropolitan cores, carpenters alone build suburbs and exurbs.[39] To the novice, the ratio of bedrooms to jobs provides a good rule of thumb to estimate at least one type of relationship between these outlying areas and their urban core.[40]

Cities_Over_750K.xls.

[36]United Nations Human Settlements, 127.

[37]Hayden, 155.

[38]Auguste C. Spectorsky, *The Exurbanites* (New York, NY: Berkley Publishing Corp, 1955), 21-23. Merriam-Webster defines exurb as the region or settlement that lies outside a city and usually beyond its suburbs and that often is inhabited chiefly by well-to-do families. Merriam-Webster Inc.

[39]Hayden, 117.

[40]Ibid., 155.

Given the complexity of modern cities, classifying them involves identifying both functional and operational relationships. For example, one can analyze a city using the simple relationship between the three developmental factors devised by the World Bank: Density, Distance, and Division.[41] Density can be simple math, as in how many humans per square foot inside a delineated urban area. Further refining that definition to a labor market capable of sustaining a large city, one over 750,000 in population, the numbers range from 44,400 people per square kilometer in Dhaka, Bangladesh to 600 people per square kilometer in Birmingham, Alabama.[42] In keeping with the theme of labor, explaining distance is a matter of differentiating between the physical distances it takes the average laborer must travel to work and the time that it takes for that laborer to do so.[43] In addition, distance can relate to the availability or access to food or water, or even essential services.[44] Simply articulated, division is the amount of economic inequity between parties that inhabit urban areas; the disparity between the haves and the have-nots.[45] One can use any of a variety of variables and coefficients to measure the amount of inequality in cities. The United Nations assigns both values and thresholds of inequality to cities, and identifies some cities as dangerous due to the level of inequity found among the populace. São Paulo, Brazil serves as a particularly striking study in contrasts (see Figure 1).

---

[41] World Bank, 6.

[42] Demographia, "Demographia World Urban Areas" http://www.demographia.com/db-worldua.pdf (2012).

[43] World Bank, 15.

[44] United States Department of Agriculture Economic Research Service, *Food Desert Locator Data* (Washington, DC: United States Department of Agriculture, 2011).

[45] United Nations Human Settlements, *State of the World's Cities 2008/2009: Harmonious Cities* (Washington, DC: Earthscan, 2008), 51.

Divisions or inequities are a common theme in current studies of urban development.[46] Often, this issue goes overlooked in relational or comparative studies. This is because aggregating the wealth of a city can provide a simple tool to relate to other cities. However, the collective flow of currency through a city only serves as one measure of its health. Taken out of context, the overall economic inputs and outputs of a city mean very little. Although there is a clear relationship between urbanization and economic growth, it is difficult to determine which came first.[47] Uneven applications of state, national, or international support and funding further

---

[46]Monty G. Marshall and Benjamin R. Cole, *Global Report 2011:Conflict, Governance, and State Fragility* (Vienna, VA: Center for Systemic Peace, 2011), 20.

[47]United Nations Human Settlements, 21.

compound this difficulty.[48] It remains that growing cities, in spite of all the sheen of prosperity, do not necessarily develop a more egalitarian distribution of wealth or income across their inhabitants.[49] Sometimes prosperity folds in on itself and an informal network encouraging further growth, employment, and sustainment occurs for reasons beyond understanding. For example, over three million people reside in Addis Ababa in Ethiopia – essentially an overgrown village given its almost complete lack of infrastructure.[50] Yet, unlike most cities, little inequity exists among the population, who all share essentially the same experience.

OPERATIONAL FRAMEWORKS AND CASE STUDIES: 1944-1969

General Harold K. Johnson, U.S. Army Chief of Staff during the buildup in Vietnam, famously said, "Where the U.S. interest requires it, that is where the Army belongs, and so far as I am concerned, that's where I am going to recommend that it go. That's our job."[51] Yet the past seventy years have left a curious void in both combat development and ground force employment: urban centers.[52] These urban centers certainly receive little attention in comparison to other aspects of ground operations. Further, the U.S. Army has operated in large cities nine times since 1944, yet there is no mention or inculcation of lessons learned from those experiences.

---

[48]World Bank, "World Development Report 2011: Conflict, Security, and Development," in *World Development Report* (Washington, DC: The World Bank, 2011).

[49]United Nations Human Settlements, 26.

[50]Ibid., 41.

[51]Graham A. Cosmas, *MAC-V: The Joint Command in the Years of Escalation, 1962-1967*, United States Army in Vietnam (Washington, DC: U.S. Army Center of Military History, 2006), 202. Transcript of briefing for USARPAC staff, 12 Mar 65, folder 5, tab 47, box 9, Johnson Papers, MHI.

[52]S.L.A Marshall, *Notes on Urban Warfare* (Aberdeen Proving Ground, MD: U.S. Army Materiel Systems Analysis Agency, 1973), 3.

Early U.S. Army doctrine did not differentiate between cities and combat fortifications in classification. At first, the U.S. Army developed doctrine for urban operations using a construct that bifurcated cities and fortified areas, but this doctrine has remained consistent in its recommendation that commanders avoid operations in either form of terrain. Less consistent is the manner in which operational planners employ their forces according to doctrine. Nevertheless, the Army often operates in urban areas, and in contrast to doctrine's consistent recommendation to avoid such terrain, operational planners have lacked consistency in their recommendations for employing forces in cities. The most common difference revolves around the option of contiguous versus non-contiguous employment. Whichever method a particular commander might choose, throughout the period since 1944, U.S. Army urban operations consistently lacked consideration of the special properties and conditions relevant to operating in large cities, where the density of infrastructure, ability of combatants to become instantly anonymous, and external dependencies on commodities create pathways of violence against and through them.[53]

FM 31-50, 1944

The U.S. Army published Field Manual 31-50, *Attack on a Fortified Position and Combat in Towns* (FM 31-50) in 1944, which went on to serve as the U.S. Army's doctrine for urban operations for the remainder of World War II. Developed and written prior to the wars in European and Pacific theaters, the U.S. Army packed the document with tactical techniques and maxims in preparation for total war. As such, some passages reflect an advanced understanding of space, while others seem naïve. The writers of the 1944 FM 31-50 delineated cities according to three typical construction types closing in on an urban core: isolated houses on the outskirts (effectively pillboxes), closely spaced semidetached houses in the interspatial areas (sites that offer cover in the central zone), and blocks of adjoining buildings of varying sizes and height in

---

[53]Graham, xxii.

an impregnable city center.[54] Because of this classification, the writers warned that, "...the final objective will probably not be houses or streets, but such strategic points as the railroad station, telephone exchange, gas and other public utility works."[55]

This important insight stood out as the first glimmer of economy of force concerns in large cities – an insight absent in subsequent manuals, at least until the twenty-first century. However keen that particular insight might have been, the document was also rife with warnings about looting and the difficulty of maintaining discipline in urban areas, admonishments that probably seemed trivial with respect to operations larger than platoon-sized efforts.[56] The 1944 FM 31-50 also invented and reinforced the narrative that occupants would evacuate urban areas when combatants arrived with the intention to fight. If residents of an urban area did not flee on their own in such an event, the manual directed U.S. Army forces to take responsibility for the timely and effective disposition of all persons unwilling or unable to contribute to friendly operations.[57]

Manila, 1944

The Sixth United States Army (6th USA) first employed this doctrine in Manila to great success in early 1945.[58] As part of a larger campaign plan, the 6th USA landed at the southern tip of the Philippine's largest and most populous island, established basing, seized Manila, and

---

[54]Department of the Army, Field Manual (FM) 31-50, *Attack on a Fortified Position and Combat in Towns*, (Washington, DC: Headquarters, Department of the Army, 1944), 62.

[55]Ibid.

[56]Ibid., 66.

[57]Ibid., 97.

[58]Robert Ross Smith, *Triumph in the Philippines*, United States Army in World War II. The War in the Pacific (Washington, DC: Office of the Chief of Military History, Dept. of the Army, 1963), 217.

awaited further instructions.[59] While the plan included a relatively simple phasing scheme, it involved a rather complex convergence of two corps and one airborne infantry division from separate directions. Further, as the 6th USA Staff wrote in its official report, "…the enemy had done everything possible to strengthen the defenses of Manila," until the last possible moment.[60] On 3 February 1945, advance elements of the 6th USA arrived at the city's outskirts to exploit the actions taken by the United States Air Corps which had, in accordance with current doctrine, isolated Manila by destroying the city's key transportation infrastructure.

Strikingly, the 6th USA then moved to a series of non-contiguous objectives, notably the water supply facilities and even eyots between key bridges.[61] After affecting enough of a presence, the corps commanders lifted restrictions on the use of their ammunition-constrained artillery, correctly assuming that the inhabitants of population Manila had already left, or were in the process of leaving.[62] Those who could not get out fast enough relied on 6th USA forces to shepherd them out of harm's way. This led to unforeseen operational pauses, which drew out the combat for longer than expected, because planners had not accounted for the mass of traffic.[63]

Regardless, the 6th USA had shocked the Japanese with the effective employment of U.S. Army doctrine - so much so that the Japanese withdrew under significant pressure on 22 February 1945, a scant ten days after the battle began.[64] The commanders of the two corps used space

---

[59]"Sixth United States Army Report on the Luzon Campaign 9 January 1945 - 30 June 1945," San Fransisco, CA, 3.

[60]Ibid., 51.

[61]Smith, 252, 262. Merriam-Webster defines eyot or ait as a little island. They are leftover piers used in pre-industrial bridge construction and are common sights in older cities. Merriam-Webster Inc.

[62]Smith, 264.

[63]Ibid., 287.

[64]"6th USA Report Vol. 1," 37.

16

brilliantly – and as described in the 1944 FM 31-50. Specifically, the 6th USA staff helped the commander array objectives in accordance with the three typical construction types found in cities – key terrain and intersections on the outskirts (up to 120 miles from the city's center), parks in the meso-city, and high-rises in the dense urban core.[65] Using this methodology, the 6th USA approached on lines of communication with workable mobility corridors, staged at Harrison Park, and then attacked the defending Japanese forces who fought viciously but ultimately culminated at the Manila Hotel in Intramuros, the cultural center of the city.[66] Other objectives "downtown" included police stations and other municipal buildings such as the hospital, the university, and City Hall.[67] This is an interesting facet of the battle for Manila: both sides fought primarily from within the protective cover of hardened municipal buildings and commercial landmarks. Although the fighting led to extensive collateral damage to civil infrastructure and housing, this did not occur intentionally. Both sides carefully targeted opposing combat formations rather than potentially decisive terrain; any damage to such terrain occurred merely because of the defenders' presence there.

Berlin and Tokyo, 1945

The U.S. Army found itself in an entirely different situation in both Berlin and Tokyo just a few months later, after the unconditional surrender of Germany and Japan. Although the population density and size of both Berlin and Tokyo at the time were comparable, the diffusion of industry and the construction materials used in the cities were vastly different, not to mention the cultural differences and demographics.[68] The presence of an adversary, the Soviet Union,

---

[65]"After Action Report: XIV Corps M-1 Operation," Manila, Phillipines, 221.

[66]"6th USA Report Vol. 1," 39.

[67]Smith, 286-288.

[68]William W. Ralph, "Improvised Destruction: Arnold, Lemay, and the Firebombing of

further complicated efforts to stabilize the city.[69] Nevertheless, Tokyo and Berlin still had much in common: each represented a destroyed vestige of empire. Political scientist Francis Fukuyama wrote: "both Germany and Japan were both very strong bureaucratic states long before the U.S. defeated them…in both countries, the state apparatus survived the war and was preserved into the postwar period with remarkably little change."[70] The strength of these longstanding and entrenched bureaucracies provided a starting point for reformation of governance.

Regardless of the relative maturity of the German state, the Allies had wracked Berlin and its population, leaving only the very old and the very young to attend to the matter of running the large city.[71] This resulted in a number of tasks that the U.S. Army had to take direct responsibility for when its forces arrived in the American sector of Berlin: from traditional constabulary concerns to public health infrastructure such as drinking water and trash removal.[72] U.S. Army operations became difficult because many operational and strategic level headquarters were rapidly shutting down since the war was "over." This meant that, upon arrival to Berlin and over the next few years, U.S. Army forces lacked large headquarters to assist in planning and resourcing even simple operations.[73] In addition to the dearth of personnel and the long list of tasks the U.S. Army had to accomplish in Berlin, there was immense pressure coming from Washington. U.S. Policymakers wanted to take the U.S. Army off its war footing as quickly as

---

Japan," *War in History* 13, no. 4 (2006): 522.

[69]Andrei Cherny, *The Candy Bombers: The Untold Story of the Berlin Airlift and America's Finest Hour* (New York, NY: Berkley Publishing Group, 2009), 96.

[70]Francis Fukuyama, *State-Building: Governance and World Order in the 21st Century* (Ithaca, NY: Cornell University Press, 2004), 38.

[71]Cherny, 94, 98.

[72]"Early Occupation Plans and Experience," Heidelberg, GER, 18.

[73]Ibid., 42.

possible. This created significant constraints, like the chronically understrength condition of the constabulary forces requested by the limited staff of U.S. Army Europe. Tellingly, these units reported at an average twenty-five percent strength, and experienced one-hundred percent annual turnover (see Figure 2).[74]

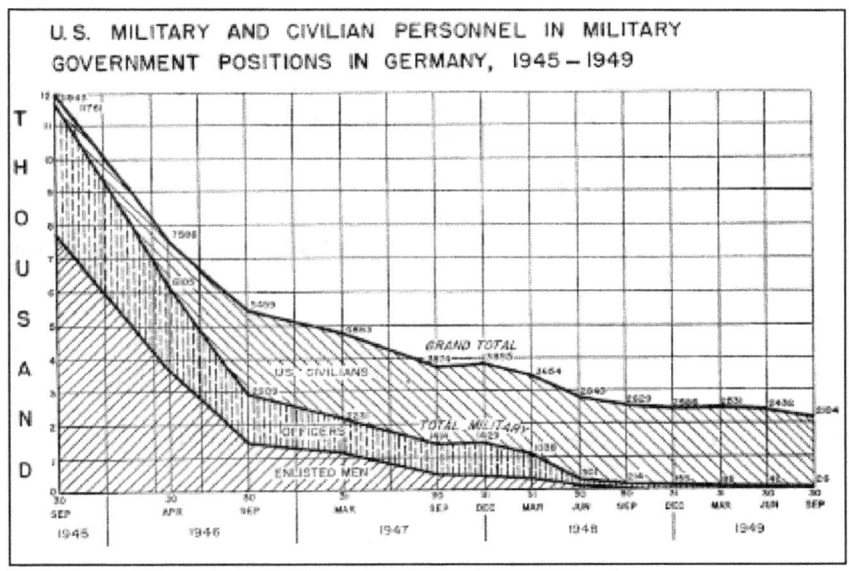

Figure 2. Berlin's military to civil transition.

Source: Historical Division, U.S. Army Europe (from the 1953 *Early Occupation Plans and Experience*).

---

[74]Kendall D. Gott, *Mobility, Vigilance, and Justice: The U.S. Army Constabulary in Germany, 1946-1953*, Global War on Terrorism Occasional Paper (Fort Leavenworth, KS: Combat Studies Institute Press, 2005), 15.

Allied bombing, artillery, and street combat effectively demolished Berlin. From a purely engineering point of view, in infrastructure alone, the explosions had left the city's very essence obliterated.[75] Both Germany's initial placement of its utilities' infrastructure, and the types of munitions that the Allies used against the city itself (as opposed to those that targeted its inhabitants) increased the damage to lines of all types.[76] Therefore, the U.S. Army had to determine requirements for and then distribute essential services, particularly food and heating fuel across strategic lines of communication. The Berlin Airlift has since become shorthand for this American effort to rescue the city just a few years after its fall. A famous exchange that illustrates how the military could pivot from combat operations to humanitarian relief appeared in Andrei Cherny's *The Candy Bombers*:

> "LeMay was a man of war, not a freight train operator; he saw his job as dropping bombs, not delivering packages. 'General, we must have a bad phone connection. It sounds like you are asking whether we have planes for carrying coal.' 'Yes,' replied Clay, annoyed. 'That's what I said. Coal.' There was a long pause on the phone before LeMay responded, 'The Air Force can deliver anything.'"[77]

While the Berlin Airlift eased food and fuel shortages, the Army still had to contend with other struggles in Berlin.

In addition to isolating the eastern partition of the city, the Soviets cut off the lines of communication between the areas that they did not administer themselves, creating obstacles for relief efforts. The Soviets invested heavily in East Berlin, assigning general officers to positions in the military administration of the city. By contrast, the U.S. Army dispatched a colonel and a few staff members to serve in Berlin. This imbalance in rank structure led to stilted negotiations between the Soviets and Americans over the simplest control measures in the city. There was also

---

[75]Jeffry M. Diefendorf, *In the Wake of War: The Reconstruction of German Cities after World War II* (New York, NY: Oxford University Press, 1993), 12.

[76]Diefendorf., 16.

[77]Cherny, 252.

a lack of German workers and machinery to do the labor necessary to restore the city; tasks like rubble clearance were self-organized and self-executed.[78] The logistics challenges, ineffective adjudications, and labor challenges compounded the reasons why the pre-war elites wanted nothing to do with the city. They left before the Soviets arrived and planned to stay far away, while the former Allies redistributed power by carving Berlin in half.[79] Once the two powers brokered a deal over the summer of 1948, the United States maintained a relatively stable environment in the half of Berlin that it administered, later named the Federal Republic of Germany. Nevertheless, the American and Soviet stabilization forces dealt with constant tensions that lasted well into the 1960s, and arguably until the end of the Cold War.[80]

Tokyo shared much in common with Berlin, although the scale of devastation in Japan was far worse. While the Allies may have wracked Berlin, they effectively leveled Tokyo. Historian Warren Kozak described post-war Tokyo in his biography of General Curtis LeMay:

> "Estimates put the number of people who died in Tokyo that night at 100,000, but the actual number can never be known. Over sixteen square miles of Tokyo—among the most densely populated sixteen square miles in the world—were destroyed. More than a million people were left homeless. Another two million people left Tokyo, not to return until after the war. The Air Force history of the war records that "the physical destruction and loss of life at Tokyo exceeded that at Rome . . . or that of any of the great conflagrations of the western world—London, 1666 . . . Moscow, 1812. . . Chicago, 1871. . . San Francisco, 1906. No other air attack of the war, either in Japan or Europe, was so destructive of life and property."[81]

---

[78]Diefendorf, 24.

[79]Diefendorf., 108.

[80]"The U.S. Army in Berlin, 1945-1961," Heidelberg, GER, 164, 111, 193.

[81]Warren Kozak, *Lemay: The Life and Wars of General Curtis Lemay* (New York, NY: Regenery Publishing, 2009), 224; Richard Rhodes, *Dark Sun: The Making of the Hydrogen Bomb* (New York, NY: Simon & Schuster, 2005), 21.

The U.S. Strategic Bombing Survey provided a more direct assessment: "Probably more persons lost their lives by fire at Tokyo in a 6-hour period than at any time in the history of man."[82] Given this environment of utter destruction and loss of life, when the U.S. ground forces arrived, they were shocked at the devastation. Despite Tokyo's appearance and the unconditional surrender of the Japanese military, there was no outpouring of sympathy from the occupier, as the ground combat to this point had been savage.[83] As such, Japan could not deny the occupation by the U.S., and the threat of the Soviets loomed, so the Japanese people were extraordinarily cooperative, adopting a sense of relief concerning reconstruction and applying a strong work ethic in support of reconstruction efforts.[84] Given the absence of any viable military threat, civil affairs rather than maneuver or operational doctrine provided the direction and guidance for most U.S. Army operations in post-war Japan. To this end, the utility of using Tokyo to explain the unique properties of a large urban environment is more a lesson in culture than geography or development.

While General Douglas MacArthur, the Supreme Commander for the Allied Powers, had a plan spanning strategy to tactics that he believed would bring the now inchoate Japan back to preeminence on the world's stage, the culture of the Japanese people provided the primary impetus that enabled a quick rebound from devastation. The Japanese were no monolith, and they are as diverse now as they ever were, but in general, their religious views and their ideas of honor enabled them to reconstruct quickly after disaster. Barbaric artifacts did manifest, however, such

[82]Kozak, 224.

[83]John W. Dower, *Embracing Defeat* (New York, NY: W.W. Norton Company, Inc., 1999), 72-80.

[84]William Manchester, *American Caesar*, Kindle ed. (Boston, MA: Little, Brown and Co, 1978), 9142.

as malnutrition, rampant prostitution, and a chaotic explosion of black markets.[85] To understand the reasons for some of these anomalous developments one must consider some of the less well-recognized factors at play. Historians often overlook religion and its role in World War II, but the preamble for both the rise of Nazism and Japanese Fascism is rooted in religious subtext.[86] Shintoism and the ideals of shame, cleanliness, continuity, and honor certainly played a huge role in the reconstruction efforts of the Japanese in Tokyo, and whatever barbarism manifested in post war Tokyo was a matter of economics.[87] Further, history finds Japanese urban development at the center of ecological and synthetic disasters quite often. From tsunamis and earthquakes to fires and nuclear contamination, Japanese urban centers are models of resilience. This is because of the use of trees as the primary building material and the tenets of minimalist design inherent in eastern worldviews. To this end, Japanese construction in all but the densest urban cores of modern Japan retains a quality of transience that allows both rapid construction and recovery from destruction.[88]

Korea, 1950

The Korean War, which started in June of 1950, was a major ground war fought while the world was still recovering from World War II. Asked by the nascent United Nations to spearhead a counteroffensive in Korea, the U.S. Army rapidly grew and deployed from Japan and the continental United States. The U.S. Army had just jettisoned its experienced ground force and had lost its operational and tactical air assets by way of legislation, most notably the National

---

[85]Dower, 121-148.

[86]Manchester, 9625.

[87]Manchester., 9508.

[88]Stephanie Kern, "Japan's Killer Quake," in *NOVA*, ed. Alan Ritsko (London, UK: PBS, 2011).

23

Security Act of 1947.[89] Therefore, the bulk of the U.S. Army was comprised of draftees that expected their lives to be part of a postwar peace dividend, not immediate and violent ground combat exacerbated by new forms of organization and role.[90] The U.S. Army's capability and composition were not the only challenges facing the United States in the Korean War. In terms of geography, Korea was at a shipping crossroads in the East China Sea; its settlements were sparse along the jagged coasts that the peninsula offers. Of all the cities in Korea, and for that matter all of East Asia, there were few strategic linchpins as great as Pusan on the southeastern tip of the peninsula. Seoul, another linchpin, but on the western median of the peninsula, was underdeveloped as a port, although Incheon, a few miles to the west of Seoul's suburbs was prime real estate for ship to shore operations.

Immediately after the North Korean Army crossed the 38th Parallel and captured Seoul, MacArthur flew a combat mission there, in person, to survey the damage. He developed his operational approach on the actual terrain just south of Seoul, when he spotted Incheon to the west.[91] MacArthur endeavored to split the North Korean Army from that axis, but did not have the combat power on hand due to political concerns.[92] He could do little but allow the North Koreans to push both the U.S. and South Korean Armies to a perimeter around Pusan. He traded space on the peninsula for time to lobby for and build his combat power. This drew the bulk of the North Korean Army into the southern part of the peninsula, where they encircled the population centers rather than occupying them. As such, while MacArthur set the conditions for

---

[89]Louis A. DiMarco, *Concrete Hell: Urban Warfare from Stalingrad to Iraq* (Oxford, UK: Osprey, 2012), 67.

[90]Allan R. Millett, *The War for Korea, 1950-1951: They Came from the North* (Lawrence, KS: University Press of Kansas, 2010), 53-56.

[91]Manchester, 11330.

[92]Ibid., 11395.

an amphibious landing in Inchon, most Korean inhabitants of Seoul remained trapped, and could not leave due to infrastructure and transportation constraints throughout the theater.[93]

By September, MacArthur had organized the X Corps, comprised of the U.S. Army's 7th Infantry Division and the Marine Corps' First Division, and placed the command of the corps under his chief of staff.[94] The X Corps was the major combat organization for Inchon, although there were complex and massive amphibious forces (Task Force 90), South Korean military forces, and air forces under the command of MacArthur.[95] They faced a reinforced division of poorly coordinated North Koreans – and although the shores of Incheon were rife with battle positions, they were unoccupied due to the radical tide shifts of the Yellow Sea.[96] It was unthinkable to North Korea that anyone would ever land at Inchon. Nevertheless, as the historian Allan R. Millett observed, the belligerents would fight on the same battlefields on the west side of Seoul as the Japanese had in Korea in the 1590s.[97] There was, to the surprise of the North Koreans, simply no other way into Seoul.

The X Corps attacked and performed the amphibious operation almost flawlessly. They were out of contact with the enemy as they phased the landing force into Incheon. The X Corps' surprise was the key to its success: the landing shocked the North Koreans so badly they could not recover.[98] X Corps entered an alien landscape on the way to Seoul. Marine Martin Russ later commented, "The condition of Seoul is a very moving sight; like a vast trash heap. A few modern

---

[93]DiMarco, 71.

[94]Ibid., 69.

[95]Millett, 243-246.

[96]Manchester, 11885.

[97]Millett, 254.

[98]T.R. Fehrenbach, *This Kind of War: A Study in Unpreparedness* (New York, NY: MacMillan, 1963), 166.

buildings, but a huge rubble of a town."[99] The Koreas had fought over Seoul twice recently, and the militarization of its natural and cultural areas showed. X Corps used a limited number of tanks in restricted terrain to break through these obstacles, leveraging key terrain and provoking counter-attacks on newly established strong points.[100] In fact, most attacks that did not use tanks failed.[101] By using armor to secure routes and facing an enemy in disarray, X Corps surrounded the city within days.[102]

South Korean Special Marines, a relatively small adjacent unit to X Corps, entered the city in order to drive the North Koreans out completely. They did so with such a retaliatory spirit that no human being, friendly, enemy, or otherwise was safe.[103] The North Koreans responded in kind, systematically killing any current or former government officials and their families.[104] They even went as far as killing anybody who spoke English before they withdrew entirely.[105] Regardless, MacArthur sped to hand over civil authority to the South Korean President as X Corps established security around Seoul in October 1950, but not necessarily inside or throughout it – there was still enough internal administration to bring Seoul back from the brink without augmentation.[106] Using Incheon and Seoul as a bridge between sea and ground lines of operation

---

[99]Martin Russ, *The Last Parallel* (New York, NY: Fromm International Publishing Corporation, 1957), 42.

[100]Millett, 255.

[101]Matthew H. Fath, "How Armor Was Employed in the Urban Battle of Seoul," *Armor* 100, no. 9 (2001): 28.

[102]Millett, 240.

[103]Fehrenbach, 166.

[104]Ibid., 168.

[105]Millett, 256.

[106]Manchester, 11946.

into the peninsula, MacArthur was now free to move and maneuver from multiple axes of advance.

FM 31-50, 1952 and FM 31-50, 1964

The U.S. Army commissioned many of the same illustrations from the 1944 version of FM 31-50 when its doctrine writers set about writing new urban manuals (see Figure 3). That, in itself, serves as a powerful allegory about the resources that went into their development. This could have meant three things: the principles of urban combat were immutable, the recent experiences of the U.S. Army in urban combat were distasteful, or this particular form of doctrine development received little effort. As such, the same material from the *1944* FM 31-50, some of it word for word, served to increase the page-count of the later versions. Urban doctrine writers captured some real world lessons from Manila and Seoul, but mostly in the allusions to planning laced throughout the documents. The lessons of Berlin and Tokyo were not included. The most striking difference between the 1944 versions and those written in 1952 and 1964 was the idea that operations in cities would or should be linear, and that the forward edge of the battlefield must be contiguous.

Figure 3. Attack from above.

Source: Illustrations by the Department of the Army in the 1944 (page 86), 1952 (page 93), and 1964 (page 42) versions of FM 31-50, from left to right. Note that the composition and framing of these images are the same.

The 1952 version of FM 31-50 was a direct reflection of the Army's experiences in Seoul. Namely, it acknowledged that transportation was not the only type of infrastructure available for movement and maneuver, stating specifically that, "…cellars, sewers, subway tunnels, thick masonry walls, and reinforced concrete floors and roofs. . ." could serve as not only pathways, but shelter and defensible positions as well.[107] The 1952 FM 31-50 also specified the deterioration of the environment in terms of rubble and debris, and its impediment on mobility – a subtlety not captured before.[108] There was a very rigid phasing construct introduced in the latter half of the manual, along with suggestions for the planner in terms of control measures. The 1952 version instructs that buildings, facilities, or centers were insufficient to determine phase lines and objectives. Instead, geometric patterns, such as streams, roads, and rail lines would determine phase lines and objectives.[109] This implies that aerial mapping would be the best planning tool, rather than the systemic and multi-source analysis used previously. The fixation with geometry was not a construct for planning purposes only. In operations, these control measures were a lock-step methodology in occupying a city, stated best by the text itself: "All enemy are cleared from each zone before resuming the attack to the next phase line."[110]

U.S. Army forces following this doctrine would clear the enemy from each zone by ensuring that "each building is thoroughly searched, that units have adequate means of communications, and that prompt resupply can be effected."[111] These three steps are nigh impossible even in a small, pacified cities – proven in all of the U.S. Army's previous

---

[107]Department of the Army, Field Manual (FM) 31-50, *Combat in Fortified Areas and Towns*, (Washington, DC: Headquarters, Department of the Army, 1952), 59.

[108]Ibid.

[109]Ibid., 76.

[110]Ibid.

[111]Ibid., 77.

experiences – yet this text appeared in the 1952 FM 31-50. This planning guidance then ceded that at a certain point, urban operations will fall to chaos, where "the fighting will resolve itself into small independent actions…and requires decentralization of control to [small unit] leaders."[112] In these types of statements, the doctrine writers of the 1952 FM 31-50 hinged an urban operation's success on planning, rather than execution, in an attempt to make sense of what MacArthur did in Seoul two years prior. There, the detailed planning of the amphibious operation informed the landing forces' sequencing into the city; the planning constructs used and the operation's stunning success may have created the confidence that cities were akin to beaches. Further, it seems that the 1952 FM 31-50 advocated taking objectives at geometric confluences in a city for the sake of "controlling" them, not for another any other purpose or effect.

The 1964 FM 31-50 continued this thread by including airborne and airmobile operations as part of the doctrinal approach to cities, and assumed that properly sequencing forces to the right objectives – planning tasks – would result in success. The 1964 version consists of many definitions, and applied taxonomy to built-up areas that assisted in planning: block-type construction, detached building areas, isolated housing areas, critical areas, and key buildings.[113] Gone was the language of aerial maps, replaced with passages such as gathering information, "…from prisoners of war, civilians, police, and utilities employees concerning unusual features of the area such as the layout of sewers and underground conduits, and vantage points for observation." [114] This was the first time urban doctrine suggested asking the locals what they think before and during operations.

---

[112]Ibid., 82.

[113]Department of the Army, Field Manual (FM) 31-50, *Combat in Fortified and Built-Up Areas*, (Washington, DC: Headquarters, Department of the Army, 1964), 27.

[114]Ibid., 29.

Figure 4. Attack through ceiling and wall.

Source: Illustrations by the Department of the Army in the 1944 (page 89), 1952 and 1964 (page 91 and 43, respectively – they use the exact same image) versions of FM 31-50, from left to right. Note the helmets and the facial characteristics of the enemy. In the 1944 version, the opposing forces are faceless Germans. In the subsequent 1952 and 1964 versions, the faces are Asian caricatures.

This was also the first time urban doctrine included the idea that the inhabitants of a city were an integral component, in themselves, to the city proper. The 1964 FM 31-50 even accounted for refugees swelling over the city's capability to sustain life – and in the same passage articulated that control of a city's citizenry was not the end in itself.[115] Rather, there was a suggestion that civil "administration" was part of operations in urban environments. In addition, there was less emphasis on detailed planning, claiming that risk is only partially offset by prescribing control measures rather than essential to success, as previous manuals had suggested.[116] To that end, the 1964 FM 31-50 made interacting with the population nearly as

---

[115]FM 31-50 (1964), 30.

[116]Ibid., 27.

important as attacking the enemy.[117] Resourced correctly, operations following the 1964 FM 31-50 planning and execution model would have accounted for large cities, because the fundamental nature of all cities is that they exist due to the efforts of inhabitants. As a secondary, but important effect, the manual drove a geographic search that played itself out in doctrine for quite some time, as the U.S. Army sought to predict where it would again face urban operations in its doctrine, and not just in intelligence collection priorities (see Figure 4).[118]

Saigon, 1968

"Within a brief 24-hour period, beginning in the early morning of January 31, the Viet Cong and North Vietnamese troops launched attacks against targets in and around Saigon, including the U.S. Embassy, Independence Palace, the Vietnamese Joint Staff Compound, the Vietnamese Naval Headquarters, the National Police Headquarters, the Saigon Radio Station and Tan Son Nhut Airport, as well as logistic, military, and government installations, throughout Gia Dinh and 31 other provinces of Vietnam. In the subsequent days of Tet, members of the enemy's military and civilian forces appeared openly in many districts and suburbs of Saigon and hamlets of Gia Dinh province."

—Victoria Pohle, RAND report for Undersecretary of Defense, International Security Affairs, published in January of 1969.

In 1968, the city of Saigon and its eleven surrounding suburbs supported approximately 2.2 million people.[119] This single district accounted for 90 per cent of South Vietnam's industrial capacity.[120] Saigon served as the seat of the state's government and its commerce. It was host to

---

[117]FM 31-50 (1964), 33.

[118]Although the 1964 FM 31-50 was not the first example of geographically based U.S. Army doctrine (best reflected by the keystone doctrine of the late 1970s and throughout the 1980s), the idea of geotypical terrain manifested itself clearly in the 1977 and 1979 urban doctrine manuals.

[119]Joseph W. Swaykos, "Operational Art in the Tet Offensive: A North Vietnamese Perspective" (Naval War College, 1996), 13. This was thirty-eight per cent of South Vietnam's population at the time.

[120]Don Oberdorfer, *Tet!* (Baltimore, MD: Johns Hopkins University Press, 1971), 125-134.

the Military Assistance Command – Vietnam (MAC-V), the major strategic headquarters for U.S. forces during the Vietnam War, as well as the U.S. Embassy. The war itself was a result of North Vietnam's desire for reunification after World War II and the continued U.S. policy of communist containment in Asia after Korea in 1953.[121] Over the course of two and a half decades, the U.S. Government struggled to deter both North Vietnam and its sponsors, China and the Soviet Union, from the horizontal or vertical escalation of the conflict while attempting to enable the Government of South Vietnam's sovereignty and overall security.[122]

As such, the war's objectives, or more aptly, limitations, confused most operational and tactical commanders; many expressed a misunderstanding or apathy towards the conflict's aims.[123] No matter the political ends, U.S. forces considered two basic operational approaches for creating political space via the ground war in Vietnam: defend Saigon proper by disrupting the North Vietnamese Army (NVA) and the Viet Cong (resident North Vietnamese sympathizers), or by primarily advising and training the Army of the Republic of Vietnam (ARVN). The commander of the MAC-V, GEN William Westmoreland, decided on the latter, and focused his efforts on the NVA line of operation into Saigon from the northern border region known as Khe Sanh.[124]

---

[121]Harold Summers, "The Strategic Perception of the Vietnam War," *Parameters* 13, no. 2 (1983): 11.

[122]Lawrence Freedman, "Escalators and Quagmires: Expectations and the Use of Force," *International Affairs* 67, no. 1 (1991): 21-28.

[123]Douglas Kinnard, *The War Managers* (Hanover, NH: University Press of New England, 1977), 24-25.

[124]Charles A. P. Turner, "Did American Leadership Fail to Correctly Heed Indications of an Impending Offensive in the Months Preceding the Tet Offensive?" (Command and General Staff College, 2003), 10.

The mission of the MAC-V steadily increased as U.S. forces poured into South Vietnam with the hope that more presence would result in more deterrence and security.[125] With this expansion came the requirement for more billets in Saigon, not only for the headquarters itself, but also for its attachments and enablers. However, security forces remained conspicuously absent. Running out of areas to house and provide workspace for staff, U.S. forces increasingly diffused into buildings throughout downtown Saigon.[126] Meanwhile, the Viet Cong (VC) presented a general threat of terrorism wherever Americans lived and worked in the city.[127] The VC represented a very real, physical threat: as early as 1964, the VC had singled out officers' quarters in Saigon and bombed them, among numerous other incidents.[128] To hedge against terrorism, U.S. forces and the ARVN worked together to emplace anti-infiltration barriers and surveillance systems in and around Saigon.[129] This partnership extended beyond operating requirements. As the sole U.S. security force in the city, the 716th Military Police Battalion emphasized their thousand-member Boy Scout troop and holiday celebrations with a sister South Vietnamese Military Police battalion in a report filed on the eve of Tet in 1968.[130]

The NVA and the VC had no plans for festivities that night. Despite signing a truce over the holiday, they mounted a coordinated assault in at least thirty-one locations across South

---

[125]Turner, 4; "The Viet Cong Tet Offensive (1968)," 21 December 1970, Saigon, Republic of Vietnam, 46.

[126]Cosmas, 268.

[127]Ibid., 273.

[128]Lewis Sorely, *Westmoreland: The General Who Lost Vietnam* (New York, NY: Houghton Mifflin Harcourt Publishing Company, 2011), 75.

[129]Turner, 5; Andrew F. Krepinevich, *The Army and Vietnam* (Baltimore, MD: Johns Hopkins University Press, 1986), 238.

[130]"Lessons Learned for the Quarterly Period Ending 31 January 1968," February 12, 1968, San Francisco, CA, 7.

Vietnam.[131] Although the exact size of the assault force is lost to the annals of war, the South Vietnamese Government estimated killing 60,000 NVA and VC combatants in South Vietnam during the battle, with another 10,000 captured.[132] In Saigon, where intelligence was easier to gather, the NVA and VC deployed approximately seventeen battalion-size elements with two division headquarters in reserve.[133] The VC aimed for the under-protected civil buildings in Saigon and mostly ignored the local population, unless they had information about their employment by the U.S. or South Vietnamese Government. When VC did find these "sympathizers" they killed them and left their corpses on the streets, sometimes with notes pinned to their bodies.[134] However, widespread terrorism against the general populace was not the order of the day.

By any measure, these tactics were effective, because over half of the inhabitants were so confused that they believed the United States and NVA were collaborating in the destruction of Saigon.[135] The sudden attacks in the city also paralyzed some inhabitants. A RAND report anecdote included an exchange between a VC and a civilian who was staring upon his approach. The VC yelled, "What do you open the door and look out for? Aren't you afraid of death?"[136] The non-combatant froze in a state of sticky fixation, attempting to pair the incongruity of violence in what had been a bustling and vibrant neighborhood.[137] Those who were not petrified in the face

---

[131]"The Viet Cong Tet Offensive (1968)," 13.

[132]Ibid., 14.

[133]Ibid., 78.

[134]Victoria Pohle, *The Viet Cong in Saigon: Tactics and Objectives During the Tet Offensive* 1969. Vol. RM-5799-ISA/ARPA. 14.

[135]Ibid., 44.

[136]Ibid., 32.

[137]Charles Fernyhough, *A Thousand Days of Wonder*, Kindle ed. (New York, NY:

of the VC flooded the streets as they evacuated to the south, especially those who feared punishment.[138] All told, the VC killed 6,300 civilians and created over 206,000 refugees.[139]

The U.S. and South Vietnamese forces had a very hard time maintaining situational awareness because of the amount of enemy activity and their poor maps of the city.[140] This rampant uncertainty facilitated the efforts of the NVA and VC, as they daringly struck at the U.S. Embassy, located in the city center.[141] In response, military police became infantryman and combat engineers in order to defend it.[142] An estimated platoon of enemy combatants fought hard against the equivalent-sized embassy security team, who was not only shocked, but also spread thin by attacks across the city.[143] The embassy security team was ultimately successful, but at a high cost both in U.S. casualties and in terms of domestic support for the war. The symbol of the embassy attack played continually on televised and print media for years – just the enemy's capability to threaten the embassy swayed much of the American public against the war.[144] Almost overnight, journalists covering Saigon started aggressively questioning U.S. service

---

Penguin Group, 2009), 555. Sticky fixation is a condition where the ". . .reflexes are trying to push [a] gaze out toward the edges, while the more practically minded cortex is trying to get [the eyes] to look at what is right in front of [them]."

[138]Pohle, 34.

[139]"The Viet Cong Tet Offensive (1968)," 57.

[140]"Special Report of Observations, Reports, and Lessons Learned During Combat Conditions 31 January to 4 February 1968," February 8, 1968. San Francisco, CA, 23.

[141]"Assault on the American Embassy: Tet, 1968," Fort McClellan, AL, 26-71.

[142]Ibid., 74.

[143]"Special Report of Observations, Reports, and Lessons Learned During Combat Conditions 31 January to 4 February 1968," 22.

[144]Peter Braestrup, *Big Story*, vol. 1 (Boulder, CO: Westview Press, 1977), 286.

members, even while they were in contact with the enemy.[145] This relatively new phenomenon

manifested itself repeatedly from Tet until the withdrawal of U.S. forces in 1975.[146]

While the attack on the embassy lasted only one day – albeit a very long one – other

combat operations in Saigon continued until April of 1968. The MAC-V sent a brigade-sized task

force to southeastern Saigon to reinforce the ARVN defensive perimeter.[147] Even in that

relatively quiet area, NVA and VC forces attempted to disrupt U.S. screening and guarding

operations until a final counter attack in late February.[148] In between these usually small but

intense engagements, civilian foot and vehicular traffic in the city was virtually non-existent;

stores, restaurants, and even schools remained closed.[149] Saigon eventually normalized into a

paradoxical combination of increased security measures and an economy centered on teeming

black markets. All the while, U.S. forces dealt with the surprise attack and its aftermath in Saigon

with no guiding doctrine or specific orders from the strategic leaders in Washington. While their

numbers continued to grow throughout South Vietnam, the U.S. Army faced steadily dwindling

domestic support after Tet because of the NVA's and VC's symbolic successes.

---

[145]"Assault on the American Embassy: Tet, 1968.," 72.

[146]Sorely, 128.

[147]"The Viet Cong Tet Offensive (1968)," 79-82.

[148]Ibid., 129.

[149]Ibid., 151-152.

OPERATIONAL FRAMEWORK: 1977-2001

As domestic support for the war waned, the quality and quantity of the U.S. Army diminished. Despite its continued engagement in Vietnam from 1969 to 1973, the U.S. Army shrunk from 1.6 million to 800,000 personnel.[150] The nature of the U.S. Army changed as well. It made the transition to an All-Volunteer Force in 1973, and became an army that was as much a personal investment on behalf of the enlistee as a profession or patriotic duty.[151] During this time of immense turbulence, GEN William E. DePuy emerged as the U.S. Army's preeminent manager of change. DePuy had two key concepts that he inculcated throughout the U.S. Army while leading the new Training and Doctrine Command, the U.S. Army's equally new doctrine clearinghouse, from 1973 until his retirement in 1977.[152] He promoted the idea that repetitive and quantifiable drills, led by non-commissioned officers and professional officers, were the key to winning battles between technological rivals.[153] Building on this basic idea, he developed the concept of "first battle," which was the maxim that U.S. Forces should achieve dominance at the outset of whatever war that they may find themselves engaged in, because wars between these technological rivals would start with little advance notice and escalate quickly.[154]

---

[150]Henry G. Cole, *General William E. DePuy: Preparing the Army for Modern War* (Lexington, KY: University Press of Kentucky, 2008), 213.

[151]Bernard Rostker, "The Evolution of the All-Volunteer Force," *Research Brief* (2006) (accessed 10 February 2013).

[152]Cole, 275. Training and Doctrine Command (TRADOC) was created by the Chiefs of Staff of the Army, GEN Westmoreland and then GEN Abrams, in 1972 when they decided that Continental Army Command should be split into Forces Command (FORSCOM) and TRADOC, thus dividing the U.S. Army into the operating and generating force that still exists in 2013.

[153]Ibid., 247.

[154]Robert A. Doughty, "The Evolution of U.S. Army Tactical Doctrine, 1946-76," *The Leavenworth Papers*, no. 1 (1979): 41. Although suprise has always been a factor in war, the 1973 Arab-Isreali War highlighted a completely different type of warfare, concurrent with Vietnam, on the world stage.

These sentiments evolved into the doctrine of "Active Defense" in the keystone Field

Manual 100-5 (FM 100-5) *Operations* of 1976, which also refocused the U.S. Army from

infantry tactics to tank and anti-tank tactics.[155] Active Defense relied on a terrain-based approach

that, in theory, would force the enemy to mass through a combination of area and mobile

defensive operations.[156] Putting primacy on the defense as the superior form of warfare was not

the only paradigm shift in the 1976 FM 100-5. Recognizing that the demands of Vietnam had

allowed a generation of weaponry to develop in the Soviet Union, the keystone doctrine for the

U.S. Army focused for the first time in a specific geographical location, the Federal Republic of

Germany, against a stated enemy, the Soviet army.[157] This allowed for an unprecedented level of

specificity in U.S. Army doctrine, demonstrated unmistakably in the urban doctrine that would

guide the force for over twenty-five years hence (see Figure. 5).[158]

---

[155]Christopher R. Gabel, *Active Defense*, ed. Roger J. Spiller, Combined Arms in Battle since 1939 (Fort Leavenworth, KS: U.S. Army Command and General Staff College Press, 1992), 92-93.

[156]Department of the Army, Field Manual (FM) 100-5, *Operations*, (Washington, DC: Headquarters, Department of the Army, 1976), 5-1 and 5-2.

[157]"From Active Defense to Airland Battle: The Development of Army Doctrine 1973-1982," June, 1984, Fort Monroe, VA, 3.

[158]Ibid., 10.". . . the manual writers included such practical reminders and precise data as seasonal mean temperatures, rainfall, and frequency of morning fog in Central Europe, as well as data about cloud layer ceilings (of interest to Cobra pilots) and 'intervisibility segments' or the average length of clear uninterrupted lines of fire characteristic of different types of terrain in West Germany."

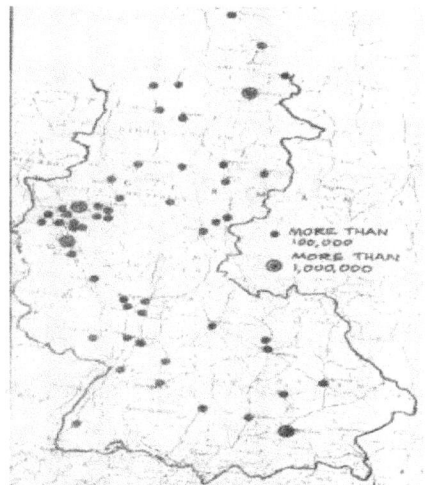 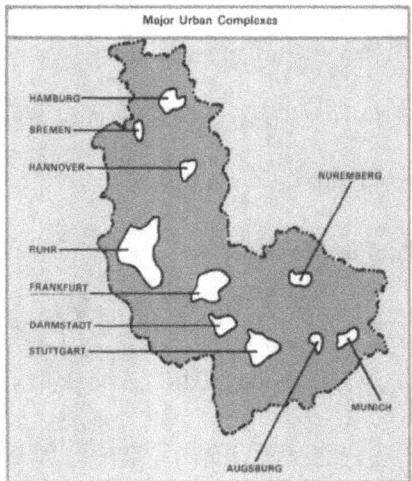

Figure 5. The German Democratic Republic and the Federal Republic of Germany.

Source: Illustrations by the Department of the Army in the 1977 (page 1-13) and the 1979 (page 1-3), versions of FM 90-10, from left to right. The illustrations in the 1977 version are hand drawn and photocopied into generally loose page setting, reflecting the impetus to get urban doctrine out immediately after the keystone FM 100-5, *Operations* of 1976.

<u>FM 90-10, 1977</u>

The 1977 version of FM 90-10, titled *Military Operations in Built-Up Areas,* or *MOBA* for short, was a marked departure from previous urban doctrine. Quantitatively, it was 340 pages in length, at least twice that of its predecessors. Qualitatively, its authors wrote it for a specific context . . . a named, and sole, theater of war: Europe. Most importantly, however, the 1977 version of FM 90-10 opened with a pronouncement regarding the inevitability of urban combat (possibly a result of the specific context of Europe envisioned by the authors). Given this inevitability, the writers included a detailed assessment – written like the intelligence preparation of the battlefield called for in the military decision making process – for every city and town in the ground chokepoint of the Fulda Gap, in line with the 1976 FM 100-5. These products included the Soviet order of battle in each location, including an N-hour sequence to help the

39

reader understand and plan for both time and effects when facing the expected enemy formations in the envisioned future conflict with the Soviet Union. In short, the authors wrote the 1977 FM 90-10 as a highly technical and descriptive document, including detailed training scenarios for mechanized division, brigade, and company-level formations. These scenarios and Soviet data have not aged well. For example, the 1977 FM 90-10 referenced the employment of tactical nuclear weapons and included an analysis of Soviet "indoctrination" methods, even identifying the number and role of political officers in each formation.[159]

The 1977 FM 90-10 did manage to achieve a certain degree of prescience regarding urban phenomenon, perhaps because of the specificity of the context for which the authors wrote it. For example, the manual included predictions such as the notion that opportunities to ". . . maneuver through the 'gaps,' or for wide sweeps around built up areas, are decreasing rapidly." This passage managed to reference both maneuver warfare theory and the conurbation of Europe in one sentence, capturing the two driving factors behind the formulation of Active Defense and its subsidiary urban doctrine.[160] In this manner, the 1977 FM 90-10 was forward-looking, but its writers also grounded it in past truths. The opening paragraphs of the document read much like the 1944, 1952, and 1964 manuals. For example, the 1977 version reinforced the maxim that most urban training occurs while in combat rather than during pre-deployment training, and warned that this is too late with respect to both mission accomplishment and risk to the soldier.[161] Other references to the manual's predecessors included lengthy sections describing building classification types and urban survivability positions.[162]

---

[159]Department of the Army, Field Manual (FM) 90-10, *Military Operations in Built-Up Areas*, (Washington, DC: Headquarters, Department of the Army, 1977), 3-19.

[160]Ibid., i.

[161]Ibid., 1.1-1.2.

[162]Ibid., A1-C22.

Although descriptive and somewhat recycled from previous efforts, the writers of the 1977 FM 90-10 interspersed significant insights into the nature of urban warfare, mostly because of its focus on real places and real threats. The following passage from the introduction provides a particularly relevant example: "Success in urban battles will frequently be measured by how well one can impose his will on the enemy with minimum destruction of structures and alienation of the population."[163] This sentence marks the first time that urban doctrine referenced military responsibilities in post-conflict conditions beyond the responsibility to enable administration. This formed a central thread in the manual because it repeatedly alluded to the complexity and sophistication of Western Europe as factors military units must consider when conducting operations. One passage in the manual described this complexity of terrain as, ". . . consist[ing] of multi-storied apartment buildings, separated by large open areas such as parking lots, recreation areas, parks and individual one story buildings."[164] Later in the manual, these cities are said to have a "...sophisticated population, which is confined to a comparatively small land area."[165] At this point, the writers of the 1977 FM 90-10 identified cities as the "hub," in Western Europe, an apparent allusion to Clausewitz' concept of center of gravity.[166] Although they do not appear to have acknowledged it, their adversary, the Soviets, believed that they would not be fighting in cities at all, but rather isolating them.[167]

---

[163]FM 90-10 (1977), 1-5.

[164]Ibid., 1-25.

[165]Ibid., 1-12.

[166]Ibid., 3-7.

[167]DiMarco, 155. As the Nazis had attempted to do to the Soviets during World War II.

41

FM 90-10, 1979

The writers of the 1979 FM 90-10 formalized the rough pagination of the 1977 manual

and refined its name to *Military Operations in Urban Terrain*, or *MOUT*, an acronym still in

common use throughout the U.S. Army. They also increased its predecessor's specificity down to

the platoon level, and added sections called "special situations" that soldiers could both easily

simulate in the field or imagine on an overhead projector. The 1979 manual again reinforced the

inevitability of combat in cities.[168] The manual's authors demonstrated their confidence in this

assertion in its opening paragraph: "Major urban areas represent the power and wealth of a

particular country in the form of industrial bases, transportation complexes, economic institutions,

and political and cultural centers."[169] In the next few paragraphs, the doctrine covers the two

essential levels of analysis in military operations, both in general and in cities themselves: the

brigade and higher commander's fight, focused on urban sprawl; and the battalion and below

commander's fight, focused on a homogenous type of urban terrain that influences the nature of

combat these smaller tactical formations waged.[170]

---

[168]Department of the Army, Field Manual (FM) 90-10, *Military Operations on Urbanized Terrain*, (Washington, DC: Headquarters, Department of the Army, 1979), 2-3.

[169]Ibid., 1-1.

[170]Ibid., i-ii.

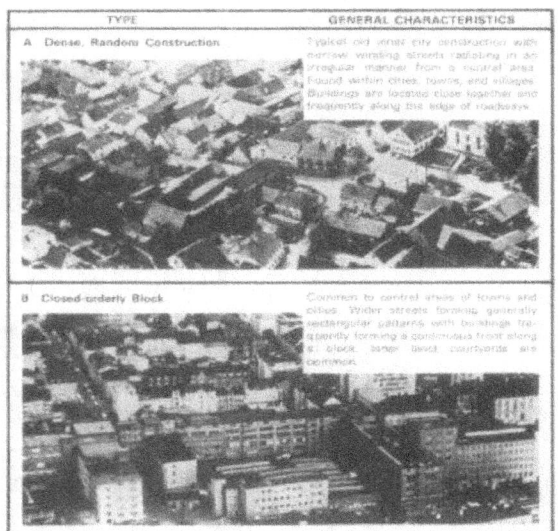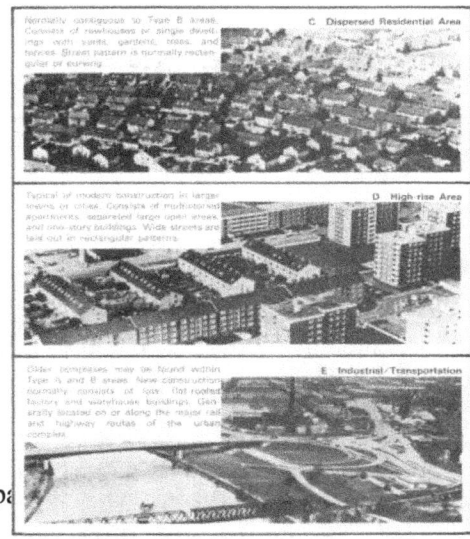

ling p

Source: Photos by the Department of the Army in the 1979 FM 90-10, pages 1-4 and 1-5. Note not only the lack of graphics, but also that these examples emphasize the characteristics of individual buildings, not their interrelationships or differences in major types. It appears that the photographer sought clean shots of specific building types rather than depictions of the relation between various building types in terms of their relationships to each other and their distance from the urban core.

Further reinforcing the idea of the Clausewitzian hub, the 1979 FM 90-10 described the decisive psychological advantage of isolating a city, while simultaneously noting that the surrounding villages and small towns would find themselves "...caught up in the battle."[171] This marked a tonal shift in the doctrine, which now reflected a sense of empathy for the urban populace in conflict. This sentiment runs consistently throughout the manual. The notion of victimhood extended to the five basic building and street patterns found throughout the world, which, as described in the manual, consisted essentially of Western Europe and its colonies (see Figure 6).[172] As it turned out, this empathy marred U.S. Army operations for nearly thirty years,

---

[171]FM 90-10 (1979), 1-1.

[172]FM 90-10 (1979), 115.

43

as the urban doctrine that informed operations from 1979 through the twenty-first century's

Global War on Terror did not account for actively or passively hostile city inhabitants. In

particular, the doctrine reflected a pervasive idea: the U.S. Army would exclusively operate in

cities with Occidental rather than Oriental denizens.[173]

CONCLUSIONS

The concept of Active Defense held sway for several years despite the lack of any

doctrinal empathy or allegiance to the urban populations of Europe. Its urban warfare component

emphasized dense random construction, closed orderly blocks, dispersed residential areas, high

rises, and industrial or transportation zones as classifications used for determining rate of march –

not an understanding of space in relation to culture – as one can see reflected in the operational

graphics used throughout the manuals.[174] That is not to say that the 1976 FM 100-5 and the 1979

FM 90-10 served a singular purpose, however. Active Defense drove capability development for

at least a decade, and MOUT provided the urban framework for the U.S. Army for 23 years. In

fact, MOUT techniques had so much utility at the tactical level that they endured through the

evolution of AirLand battle in the 1982 version of FM 100-5 and remained consistent in every

keystone doctrinal manual thereafter.[175]

Panama City, 1989

A decade after the publication of the 1979 FM 90-10, the U.S. Army found itself in need

of doctrine for another large city, Panama City.[176] The U.S. Army had stationed troops in the

---

[173]Edward W. Said, *Orientalism*, Vintage Books ed. (New York, NY: Random House, 1994), 31-35.

[174]Mostly, these graphics were depictions of axes of advance or avenues of approach.

[175]Gabel, 95.

[176]Ronald H. Cole, Operation Urgent Fury: The Planning and Execution of Joint

44

country of Panama, much like The Federal Republic of Germany, for quite some time – in fact,

the U.S. presence in Panama stretched back to the construction of the Panama Canal at the turn of

the century. In support of this forward stationing, leaders there naturally tailored doctrine and

training for the operational environment of South America. In addition, to offset the European

focus of the keystone doctrine of AirLand battle, select U.S. Army forces stationed in the United

States trained using "The Cuban Handbook" at the Joint Readiness Training Center, reflecting a

strategic hedge.[177] Both this handbook and the localized training focused on the enemy's order of

battle in open fields or the jungle, not in urban areas, much less the large cities in the southern

hemisphere.

When the National Command Authority (NCA) directed the U.S. Southern Command to

"…safeguard the lives of Americans, to defend democracy in Panama, to combat drug trafficking,

and to protect the integrity of the Panama Canal treaty" because of a diplomatic breakdown, most

of the apportioned U.S. Army forces transitioned to combat operations seamlessly on 19

December 1989.[178] This was limited to the countryside of Panama at first.[179] As such,

conventional units were able to reconnoiter and rehearse seizing their objectives in plain sight.[180]

Operations in Grenada 12 October - 2 November 1983 (Washington, DC: Office of the Chairman of the Joint Chiefs of Staff, 1997), 5; Timothy J. Geraghty, "25 Years Later: We Came in Peace," Proceedings 134, no. 1268 (2008). Although not occuring in large cities, operations in Beirut and Grenada came with hard lessons concerning force protection and joint interoperability that colored all operations from 1983 on.

[177]Robert M. Cronin, "JRTC to Just Cause: A Case Study in Light Infantry Training" (Study, U.S. Army War College, 1991), 4.

[178]Ronald H. Cole, *Operation Just Cause: The Planning and Execution of Joint Operations in Panama February 1988 - January 1990* (Washington, DC: Office of the Chairman of the Joint Chiefs of Staff, 1995), 32-33. Steven W. Senkovich, "From Port Salines to Panama City: The Evolution of Command and Control in Contingency Operations" (United States Army Command and General Staff College, 1991), 35.

[179]Senkovich, 36.

[180]"Operation Just Cause: The Incursion into Panama," Washington, DC, 12-14. Many

Later, the President ordered the immediate apprehension and extradition of Manuel Noriega, the de facto ruler of Panama, which required elements to operate in Panama City.[181]

The 193d Infantry Brigade, already forward stationed in Panama but acquiring subordinate units from all over the continental United States during the deployment process, served as the lead formation attacking into the city.[182] Although the 193d executed only one component of many in a very complex plan, it sought to secure several key objectives in Panama City: physically and psychologically important government buildings. In this manner, the 193d performed a unique mission; one designed to shock the government of Panama into handing over Noriega. Combat operations, in which U.S. forces performed with great success, did not last long; most units – including the 193d – transitioned to stability operations within four days.[183] As such, operations in Panama City, from D-day to redeployment, serve as a synthesis of the preceding forty-five years of doctrinal and experiential lessons learned, regardless of temporal sequencing.

The 193d shared many experiences in common with its predecessors in large city operations since World War II. As in Manila, the battles occurred over government buildings in the highly populated downtown area of Panama City. Like Berlin, another immediate drawdown ensued, as public support waned and the NCA declared the war "over."[184] Resembling Tokyo,

---

units were aware of the deteriorating conditions and began local rehearsals.

[181]Ibid., 9.

[182]Ibid., 19; Senkovich, 37-38. The 193d, a light infantry brigade headquarters charged with operations throughout Panama prior to the failed coup in 1988, organized as "Task Force Bayonet" before and during Operation Just Cause. Markedly, planners reinforced the task force with several military police companies, a mechanized infantry battalion, and a light tank platoon, among other units before combat operations began.

[183]John S. Brown, *Kevlar Legions* (Washington, DC: U.S. Army Center of Military History, 2012), 52. This is because the majority of the Panamanian people greeted U.S. forces as "liberators," and also because the U.S. Army forces had many soliders who spoke Spanish in thier ranks, easing relations.

[184]Cole, *Operation Just Cause: The Planning and Execution of Joint Operations in*

many previous foes had to reintegrate themselves as part of the police force, among other services.[185] Almost identically to Seoul, armored vehicles had to crush or sweep away vehicles and debris.[186] Similar to both Seoul and Saigon, as enemy units or groups retreated, they set fires in order to create a flood of refugees to cover their withdrawal.[187] In another similarity with U.S. Army operations in Saigon, military personnel regularly interfaced with the press during operations.[188] Significantly, one common thread ran through all of these operations: although the U.S. Army had adapted its training plans to the requirements of the 1979 FM 90-10, *MOUT* training consisted simply of clearing a few small buildings on unobstructed streets. It did not include any simulation of the roadblocks, rubble, refugees, snipers, or fifteen-story apartment complexes associated with large cities.[189] Once again, U.S. Army forces learned how to conduct urban combat in large cities under actual combat conditions, rather than during pre-deployment training.

Despite the frequency of previous experiences of U.S. Army forces in large cities, some factors did make operations in Panama City during Operation Just Cause truly different from earlier urban operations. Helicopters added a new dimension of mobility, and in a sense, vulnerability, throughout the city.[190] Senior leaders withheld indirect fire authorities at the battalion-commander level as a risk mitigation measure, and in Panama City proper, only a

---

Panama February 1988 - January 1990, 68.

[185]"Operation Just Cause: The Incursion into Panama," 43.

[186]Ibid., 24.

[187]Ibid., 25.

[188]Steven N. Collins, "Just Cause Up Close: A Light Infantryman's View of [Low Intensity Conflict]," *Parameters* 22, no. 2 (1992): 63.

[189]"Operation Just Cause: The Incursion into Panama," 45.

[190]Cronin, 18; DiMarco, 186.

division commander could authorize indirect fire.[191] Such restrictions were relatively new. The civilian population of Panama City also reacted to combat in a unique way. While most refugees sped to get away from whatever violence was occurring, some stayed – but not as spectators. A subset of the population took advantage of the lull in civil authority and looted whatever they could get their hands on.[192]

Finally, and for complex reasons, U.S. Army forces expected the U.S. Embassy in Panama to assume responsibility for post-combat operations.[193] This marked the first time that the U.S. State Department performed duties of this kind in a large city, and it marked the rejection of the idea that combat and civil authority must operate in tandem and in an integral fashion to conduct effective urban operations.[194] The process of intelligence compartmentalization compounded this issue. In the interest of maintaining operational security, the NCA did not inform other executive agencies of its operations. This led to significant challenges during later developmental efforts.[195] Operational security did not just cloud the inter-organizational effort, however. Battalion commanders preparing for deployment in the United States did not receive the geospatial products they needed for planning and training until the very last minute.[196] Once operating in Panama, units experienced a consistent dearth of intelligence; what few products

---

[191]Cole, *Operation Just Cause: The Planning and Execution of Joint Operations in Panama February 1988 - January 1990*, 23, 41.

[192]Richard H. Shultz, *In the Aftermath of War: United States' Support for Reconstruction and Nation-Building in Panama Following Just Cause* (Maxwell Air Force Base, AL: Airpower Research Institute, 1993), 28.

[193]Ibid., 24.

[194]Schadlow, "War and the Art of Governance," 86.

[195]Shultz, 18. "Operation Just Cause: The Incursion into Panama," 46.

[196]Cronin, 6.

48

existed rarely made it down to the units themselves – even during the transition to stability operations.[197]

Although Manual Noriega himself stated that "…the invasion and its effect and consequence of death have no real legacy or messages for any class of students; it could only serve to create or feed an appetite for sadism and cruelty that serves no purpose," history shows that the operation turned out quite differently.[198] Panama serves as a well suited, albeit short, example of what the U.S. Army typically experiences in large cities, and especially so in the time period from 1944 to the Global War on Terror. For many of the participants, their experiences in Panama seemed new, but the Army had fought in such situations before – it simply had not captured the lessons it learned in those situations in its operational doctrine.

Trends

The U.S. Army experienced a recurrence of these new experiences just a few years later in Mogadishu, which was not a large city in 1993 (it did not have a population of 750,000 or more), but manifested some important aspects of urban operations nonetheless, particularly in the vulnerability of helicopters in urban areas.[199] The activities and attributes of the operation in Mogadishu gave it a unique character, such as the driving force of U.S. reluctance to engage in long-term nation-building operations.[200] Other manifestations included the population's tendency to collude with the enemy for fear of retribution through activities like setting fires to signal trouble, using women and children as human shields, or creating chaos in the streets during U.S.

---

[197]Ibid., 7.

[198]Manuel Noriega, "Interview Concerning Just Cause," ed. Fernando Guadalupe (Fort Leavenworth, KS: School of Advanced Military Studies, 2007).

[199]DiMarco, 186.

[200]Richard W. Stewart, "The United States Army in Somalia, 1992-1994," ed. U.S. Army Center for Military History (Fort Leavenworth, KS: 2002), 6.

forces' offensive operations.[201] In this sense, urban centers, whether considered large cities or not, often display characteristics that one would consider far from "Occidental." Confronted with this alien landscape, U.S. Army forces began integrating "force protection" in their planning, while allocating ever fewer forces into urban areas, a trend that continued throughout the Global War on Terror.[202]

No one entity or discipline can understand or explain all of the complex characteristics of large cities, even outside of a military context – only synthesis of historical lessons can offer a glimpse of what truly takes place when the U.S. Army operates within them. Nevertheless, urban operations, and especially those occurring in large cities, merit further study. Not only do large cities invite pathways of violence against and through them, but also the U.S. Army historically operates in one every seven to ten years.[203] In Manila, the civilian population density created impassible urban terrain. In Berlin, a massive and competitive relief and reconstruction effort began even as the U.S. populace turned its attention to domestic affairs. In Tokyo, the U.S. Army helped a culture rebuild as it dealt with the acceptance of defeat, but it benefited from Japan's historically superior construction methods, which assisted greatly in reconstruction. In Seoul, the U.S. Army confronted timeless strategic geography in the same manner that combatants had 500 years earlier, proving that infrastructure, especially aged infrastructure, exists in specific places for good reasons. In Saigon, the lack of security forces and the rapid increase in the cycle of violence resulted in an amplified significance of the attack on the U.S. Embassy to the American people. In Panama City, new phenomena added additional complexity to operations in large

---

[201]Mark Bowden, *Black Hawk Down: A Story of Modern War*, Kindle ed. (New York: Atlantic Monthly Press, 1999), 205-210; 778-835.

[202]Robert F. Baumann and Lawrence A. Yates with Versalle F. Washington, *My Clan against the World*, ed. Lawyn C. Edwards, Military Case Studies (Fort Leavenworth, KS: Combat Studies Institute Press, 2003), 2.

[203]Graham, xxii.

cities, including the employment of helicopters by U.S. Army forces and the population's reaction to the violence, which atypically included widespread looting (a phenomenon seen far more frequently after Panama than before). Panama City also represents two modern trends: the tyranny of classification in a U.S. whole-of-government approach, as well as bureaucratic realities limiting the effectiveness of executive agencies.

Recent U.S. Army, Joint, and Departmental Efforts

One can see the driving idea behind the narrative of the 2002 Joint Publication 3-06, *Joint Urban Operations* (JP 3-06) in the following quote: ". . . human intelligence and an understanding of the social and political fabric of the area **may** outweigh technical means of gathering information."[204] The word "may" appeared in bold type here, and the writers sought to convey the same sentiment throughout the rest of the publication. In this first effort to produce a joint publication containing urban operational doctrine, the writers called for these socio-political maps down to the lowest level. They emphasized the value of three-dimensional imagery, implying that such technology all but guaranteed success.[205] Nonetheless, the publication listed a series of criteria for the reader to consider before undertaking urban operations. Each criteria individually, and the assessment they enabled collectively led the reader to see the wisdom in avoidance of urban terrain whenever possible.[206]

Both the 2003 and 2006 iterations of the U.S. Army's Field Manual 3-06, *Urban Operations* (FM 3-06) highlighted the impossibility of ascribing specific doctrinal solutions to the

---

[204]The Joint Staff, Joint Publication (JP) 3-06, *Joint Urban Operations*, (Washington, DC: Headquarters, The Joint Staff, 2002), ii-4.

[205]JP 3-06 (2002), iii-12.

[206]Ibid., iii-1 and iii-2.

full range of potential urban situations.[207] The doctrine writers suggested that terrain, infrastructure, and society made up a dynamic system, and that the U.S. Army must learn and then manipulate key facilities within that system.[208] As insightful as that construct appeared, the first step in analysis simply involved gathering as many maps and overlays as possible in order to garner understanding and appreciation, reflecting the emphasis on technological solutions to U.S. military problems so prevalent in recent years.[209] Despite the emphasis on technological innovations, the 2003 version of the manual also seemed regressive in many ways. For example, its authors asserted that ". . . well-trained, dismounted infantry units," would carry the day in all types of urban operations – a view that history has repeatedly proven wrong – combined arms teams remain the most effective force designs for urban operations.[210] Leaving that idea aside, the 2006 version of FM 3-06 included the idea of U.S. Army personnel working together formally and informally with governmental and non-governmental organizations, and it emphasized the need to preserve critical infrastructure during combat operations.[211] A supporting manual, the 2008 Field Manual 2-91.4, *Intelligence Support to Urban Operations* (FM 2-91.4) devoted 150 pages to information that would help soldiers identify this critical infrastructure, albeit with no prioritization.[212]

The 2009 Joint Publication 3-06, *Joint Urban Operations* (JP 3-06) acknowledged on the first page of the manual that – contrary to what the U.S. military advertised or policymakers

---

[207]Department of the Army, Field Manual (FM) 3-06, *Urban Operations*, (Washington, DC: Headquarters, Department of the Army, 2003), 1-1.

[208]Ibid., 2-2.

[209]Ibid., b-18.

[210]Ibid., 4-3.

[211]FM 3-06 (2006), 6-2; 6-12 and 6-13.

[212]FM 2-91.4 (2008), 1-20.

believed – U.S. ground forces usually found themselves operating in large cities.[213] The writers

then identified the most important aspects of urban operations: the ability to learn and adapt.[214]

They explained the preeminence of these factors by pointing out that cities were "…human built

for human purposes," and they have a rhythm and pattern that resists static or isolated

representation.[215] Even more strikingly, the manual included the admission that, "Operations in a

single phase are unlikely to prove decisive in a [Joint Urban Operation] . . . backward planning

from enable civil authority is critical in this regard."[216]

    This opinion led to changes in departmental efforts and policies almost immediately. The

Peacekeeping and Stability Operations Institute had multiple executive agencies sign its 2009

Guiding Principles for Stabilization and Reconstruction, which contained two central tenets

concerning large cities: only act after achieving an understanding of local context, and remember

that large cities tend to grow even larger when people go there in search of government

assistance.[217] The United States Agency for International Development has an even simpler

model, devised in 2010, that helps a U.S. ground force operating in large cities, which involves

asking inhabitants two simple questions: "Who do you believe can solve your problems, and what

should be done first?"[218] Nevertheless, these recent publication still lack any direct references to

---

[213]JP 3-06 (2009), I-1.

[214]Ibid., I-11.

[215]Ibid., II-1, II-2, and II-15.

[216]Ibid., iii-20.

[217]United States Army Peacekeeping and Stability Operations Institute, *Guiding Principles for Stablization and Reconstruction*, (Carlisle, PA: United States Institute of Peace, 2009), 6-39 and 10-185.

[218]United States Agency for International Development, Office of Military Affairs, *Stabilization and the District Stability Framework*, (Washington, DC: U.S. Agency for International Development, 2010), 35-36.

large cities or their significant uniqueness when compared to smaller urban centers. Despite all of the recent U.S. Army, joint and departmental staff work, the output serves merely as tools to integrate into the understanding process.

Another way exists to evaluate urban environments, and especially large cities, termed by

urban theorist Phil Hubbard as the tension between pathologies and ecologies (see Figure 7).[219]

Despite its forward thinking nature, the 2009 JP 3-06 still contained the passage: "poor urban

areas…are also breeding grounds for extreme political and terrorist movements."[220] While this

may be true in some cases, such statements reflect an inability to recognize the significant

opportunity present in large cities. In fact, most of the doctrinal efforts concerning cities assume

that any U.S. Army operations in a city will begin in an urban environment fundamentally and

perhaps irreparably broken before the first unit's arrival. For example, the 2010 *Joint Operating*

Environment, which serves as the environmental frame for U.S military capability development to

at least 2018, includes the following statement:

> "With so much of the world's population crammed into dense urban areas and
> their immediate surroundings, future Joint Force Commanders will be unable to evade
> operations in urban terrain. The world's cities, with their teeming populations and slums,
> will be places of immense confusion and complexity, physically as well as culturally.
> They will also provide prime locations for diseases and the population density for
> pandemics to spread."[221]

While the tone of this environmental frame helps identify threats so that capability gaps are

identified, the same cities castigated in this passage as places to avoid represent highly significant

cultural centers to their indigenous populations that offer continuity and meaning to countless

human beings.

Dr. Richard Norton, a Naval War College professor, exemplified the pathological view of

cities in his 2003 article published by the Naval War College review: "The vast size of a feral

---

[219]Phil Hubbard, *City* (New York, NY: Routledge, 2006), 26.

[220]JP 3-06 (2009), ii-8.

[221]Joint Forces Command Joint Futures Group, *The Joint Operational Environment*,
(Norfolk, VA: The Joint Staff, 2010), 57.

city', he argued, 'with its buildings, other structures, and subterranean spaces, would offer nearly perfect protection from overhead sensors, whether satellites or unmanned aerial vehicles."[222] While the idea is vaguely threatening in its own right, Norton goes further in introducing a simple construct with which to classify cities.[223] He argues that by using a simple three-by-three grid, one can classify all cities as either healthy, marginal, or going feral.[224] This construct has found its way into multiple academic and defense discussions as an impetus for action. When accompanied by the cultural displays of a city's former glory, the pathological view of a city beings to seep into almost all judgment concerning cities. Anthropologist Joanne Sharp explained that these older depictions of cities ". . . overwhelm the viewer with ruined greatness and an implied criticism of the local people for neglecting their own monuments so that architecture falls into decay."[225] This feeds into the perception that the civilians in urban centers are hopeless, which is of great utility when prosecuting violence against them, on purpose or accidentally.[226]

The ecological view of cities stresses empowerment and reclamation over victimhood and neglect. Barry Hart, an expert in conflict and trauma, wrote, ". . . responses to humanitarian emergencies, whether in the context of war or natural disaster, involve efforts to reassure all involved that normal life is still possible." This idea neatly summarizes the ecological view of cities – both in and out of crisis.[227] Therefore, the perception of a city in crisis lies in the eye of

---

[222]Richard J. Norton, "Feral Cities," *Naval War College Review* 56, no. 4 (2003): 99-100.

[223]Graham, 55; Norton, "Feral Cities," 99-100.

[224]Norton, "Feral Cities," 101.

[225]Sharp, 24.

[226]Daniel Rothbart and K. V. Korostelina, *Why They Die: Civilian Devastation in Violent Conflict* (Ann Arbor, MI: University of Michigan Press, 2011), 11.

[227]Barry Hart, *Peacebuilding in Traumatized Societies* (Lanham, MD: University Press of America, 2008), 68.

the beholder, and while the perception of chaos in a large city may seem overwhelming at first, one can usually link such a perception to superficial or cursory observation.[228] An ecological perspective requires patience, because despite the temptation to use maps solely as a means to decipher a large city, maps merely represent an arbitrary assemblage of information, filled with the bias and purpose of the cartographer's imprint.[229] As far as U.S. Army operations are concerned, planners and leaders must understand that conflict resolution in and throughout an urban area must spring from within the city itself; military force can only create the space within which the populace can accomplish this aim.[230]

Ecological viewpoints have a complex relationship with cartography. While direct representations of an urban area, and especially a large city, have utility in terms of understanding interior and exterior space, the semantics of naming, and the extent to which cartographers use widely accepted names for the various places in the city have equal importance.[231] For example, tourist or mass transit maps may offer a better guide to determine what spaces carry the greatest significance in a city than one-meter color satellite imagery – particularly when one wants to understand these factors from the perspective of the inhabitants and their cultural imperatives.[232] An ecological view also offers insight into the commonality of large cities, despite their

---

[228]Stathis N. Kalyvas, *The Logic of Violence in Civil War* (New York, NY: Cambridge University Press, 2006), 70-71.

[229]Rebecca Solnit, *Infinite City: A San Francisco Atlas* (Berkeley, CA: University of California Press, 2010), 1.

[230]Michael V. Bhatia, *War and Intervention: Issues for Contemporary Peace Operations* (Bloomfield, CT: Kumarian Press, Inc., 2003), 130.

[231]David Newman, *Boundaries, Territory and Postmodernity*, Case Studies in Geopolitics (Portland, OR: F. Cass, 1999), 3-4.

[232]Hubbard, 78-79; Gilbert and Henderson, *London and the Tourist Imagination*, ed. David Gilbert, Imagined Londons (Albany, NY: State University of New York Press, 2002), 121-136.

Occidental or Oriental propensity, as Lewis Mumford, one of the first metropolitan researchers wrote:

> "The persistence of these overgrown containers would indicate that they are concrete manifestations of the dominant forces in our present civilization; and the fact that the same signs of overgrowth and overconcentration exist in 'communist' Soviet Russia as in 'capitalist' United States shows that these forces are universal ones, operating almost without respect to the prevailing ideology or ideal goals."[233]

Mumford meant that, despite all of the differences in the world's various cultures, large cities typically display significant similarities to each other in terms of layout and construction, and they hold essentially the same meaning to their inhabitants. They reflect of the human need for symbolic structure and continuity, and therefore, have unique properties of their own that defy matrices, geospatial maps, or other taxonomy.

---

[233]Mumford, *The City in History: Its Origins, Its Transformations, and Its Prospects*, 525-526.

BIBLIOGRAPHY

Berger, Samuel R., Brent Scowcroft, William L. Nash and Council on Foreign Relations. *In the Wake of War: Improving U.S. Post-Conflict Capabilities; Report of an Independent Task Force Sponsored by the Council on Foreign Relations* Independent Task Force Report. New York: Council on Foreign Relations, 2005.

Beyerchen, Alan. "Clausewitz, Nonlinearity, and the Unpredictability of War." *International Security* 17, no. 3 (1992): 59-90.

Bhatia, Michael V. *War and Intervention: Issues for Contemporary Peace Operations.* Bloomfield, CT: Kumarian Press, Inc., 2003.

Bowden, Mark. *Black Hawk Down: A Story of Modern War.* Kindle ed. New York: Atlantic Monthly Press, 1999.

Braestrup, Peter. *Big Story.* Vol. 1. Boulder, CO: Westview Press, 1977.

Brown, John S. *Kevlar Legions.* Washington, DC: U.S. Army Center of Military History, 2012.

Calvino, Italo. *Invisible Cities.* New York, NY: Houghton Mifflin Harcourt Publishing, 1972.

Campbell, David P. Auerswald and Colton C. *Congress and the Politics of National Security.* New York, NY: Cambridge University Press, 2012.

Cherny, Andrei. *The Candy Bombers: The Untold Story of the Berlin Airlift and America's Finest Hour.* New York, NY: Berkley Publishing Group, 2009.

Cole, Henry G. *General William E. DePuy: Preparing the Army for Modern War.* Lexington, KY: University Press of Kentucky, 2008.

Cole, Monty G. Marshall and Benjamin R. *Global Report 2011:Conflict, Governance, and State Fragility.* Vienna, VA: Center for Systemic Peace, 2011.

Cole, Ronald H. *Operation Just Cause: The Planning and Execution of Joint Operations in Panama February 1988 - January 1990.* Washington, DC: Office of the Chairman of the Joint Chiefs of Staff, 1995.

Cole, Ronald H. *Operation Urgent Fury: The Planning and Execution of Joint Operations in Grenada 12 October - 2 November 1983.* Washington, DC: Office of the Chairman of the Joint Chiefs of Staff, 1997.

Collins, Steven N. "Just Cause Up Close: A Light Infantryman's View of [Low Intesity Conflict]." *Parameters* 22, no. 2 (1992): 10.

Cosmas, Graham A. *MAC-V: The Joint Command in the Years of Escalation, 1962-1967* United States Army in Vietnam. Washington, DC: U.S. Army Center of Military History, 2006.

Cronin, Robert M. "JRTC to Just Cause: A Case Study in Light Infantry Training." Study, U.S. Army War College, 1991.

Demographia, "Demographia World Urban Areas" http://www.demographia.com/db-worldua.pdf (2012).

Department of Defense. Department of Defense Directive (DoDD) 5100.01, *Functions of the Department of Defense and Its Major Components*. Washington, DC: The Department of Defense, 2010.

Department of the Army. Field Manual (FM) 31-50, *Attack on a Fortified Position and Combat in Towns*. Washington, DC: Headquarters, Department of the Army, 1944.

Department of the Army. Field Manual (FM) 31-50, *Combat in Fortified Areas and Towns*. Washington, DC: Headquarters, Department of the Army, 1952.

Department of the Army. Field Manual (FM) 31-50, *Combat in Fortified and Built-Up Areas*. Washington, DC: Headquarters, Department of the Army, 1964.

Department of the Army. Field Manual (FM) 100-5, *Operations*. Washington, DC: Headquarters, Department of the Army, 1976.

Department of the Army. Field Manual (FM) 90-10, *Military Operations in Built-Up Areas*. Washington, DC: Headquarters, Department of the Army, 1977.

Department of the Army. Field Manual (FM) 90-10, *Military Operations on Urbanized Terrain*. Washington, DC: Headquarters, Department of the Army, 1979.

Department of the Army. Field Manual (FM) 3-06, *Urban Operations*. Washington, DC: Headquarters, Department of the Army, 2003.

Department of the Army. Field Manual (FM) 3-06, *Urban Operations*. Washington, DC: Headquarters, Department of the Army, 2006.

Department of the Army. Field Manual (FM) 2-91.4, *Intelligence Support to Urban Operations*. Washington, DC: Headquarters, Department of the Army, 2008.

Department of the Army. Army Doctrine and Training Publiciation (ADP) 5-0, *the Operations Process*. Washington, DC: Headquarters, Department of the Army, 2012.

Diefendorf, Jeffry M. *In the Wake of War: The Reconstruction of German Cities after World War II*. New York, NY: Oxford University Press, 1993.

DiMarco, Louis A. *Concrete Hell: Urban Warfare from Stalingrad to Iraq*. Oxford, UK: Osprey, 2012.

Dio, Cassius. *Roman History, Volume VII, Books 56-60*. Translated by Cary. Earnest. Vol. VII Loeb Classical Library, Edited by G.P. Goold. Suffolk, UK: St. Edmundsbudy Press, 2000.

Dolman, Everett C. *Pure Strategy: Power and Principle in the Space and Information Age*. New York, NY: Frank Cass, 2005.

Doughty, Robert A. "The Evolution of U.S. Army Tactical Doctrine, 1946-76." *The Leavenworth Papers*, no. 1 (1979): 63.

Dower, John W. *Embracing Defeat.* New York, NY: W.W. Norton Company, Inc., 1999.

Eberhart, Mark E. *Why Things Break: Understanding the World by the Way It Comes Apart.* 1st ed. New York, NY: Harmony Books, 2003.

Economic Research Service, United States Department of Agriculture. *Food Desert Locator Data.* Washington, DC: United States Department of Agriculture, 2011.

Eggleton, Art. *Report of the Somalia Comission of Inquiry* 1997. Vol. 1.

Emerson, Ralph Waldo, Waldo Emerson Forbes and Edward Waldo Emerson. *Journals of Ralph Waldo Emerson, with Annotations.* Boston, MA: Houghton Mifflin, 1909.

Fath, Matthew H. "How Armor Was Employed in the Urban Battle of Seoul." *Armor* 100, no. 9 (2001): 5.

Fehrenbach, T.R. *This Kind of War: A Study in Unpreparedness.* New York, NY: MacMillan, 1963.

Fernyhough, Charles. *A Thousand Days of Wonder.* Kindle ed. New York, NY: Penguin Group, 2009.

Freedman, Lawrence. "Escalators and Quagmires: Expectations and the Use of Force." *International Affairs* 67, no. 1 (1991): 16.

Fukuyama, Francis. *State-Building: Governance and World Order in the 21st Century.* Ithaca, NY: Cornell University Press, 2004.

Funkhouser, Anthony C. "An Assessment of the IPB Process at the Operational Level." U.S. Army Command and General Staff College, 1999.

Gabel, Christopher R. *Active Defense* Combined Arms in Battle since 1939, Edited by Roger J. Spiller. Fort Leavenworth, KS: U.S. Army Command and General Staff College Press, 1992.

Geraghty, Timothy J. "25 Years Later: We Came in Peace." *Proceedings* 134, no. 1268 (2008).

Goldratt, Eliyahu M. and Jeff Cox. *The Goal: A Process of Ongoing Improvement.* Kindle ed. Great Barrington, MA: North River Press, 2004.

Gott, Kendall D. *Mobility, Vigilance, and Justice: The U.S. Army Constabulary in Germany, 1946-1953* Global War on Terrorism Occasional Paper. Fort Leavenworth, KS: Combat Studies Institute Press, 2005.

Graham, Stephen. *Cities Under Siege: The New Military Urbanism.* London, UK: Verso, 2010.

Haitian Institute of Statistics and Information, "The Republic of Haiti Administrative Units," in *HTML table*, http://www.ihsi.ht/. Port Au Prince, Haiti: Ministry of Economy and Finance, 2009.

Hart, Barry. *Peacebuilding in Traumatized Societies*. Lanham, MD: University Press of America, 2008.

Hayden, Dolores. *Building Suburbia: Green Fields and Urban Growth, 1820-2000*. New York, NY: Pantheon Books, 2003.

Henderson, Fiona, and Gilbert, David. *London and the Tourist Imagination* Imagined Londons, Edited by David Gilbert. Albany, NY: State University of New York Press, 2002.

Herbst, Jeffrey Ira. *States and Power in Africa: Comparative Lessons in Authority and Control* Princeton Studies in International History and Politics. Princeton, NJ: Princeton University Press, 2000.

Historical Division, U.S. Army Europe, "Early Occupation Plans and Experience," Heidelberg, GER.

Hubbard, Phil. *City*. New York, NY: Routledge, 2006.

Johnson, Thomas L. and Mary R. Himes, "Assault on the American Embassy: Tet, 1968," Fort McClellan, AL.

Joint Forces Command Joint Futures Group. *The Joint Operational Environment*. Norfolk, VA: The Joint Staff, 2010.

Kalyvas, Stathis N. *The Logic of Violence in Civil War*. New York, NY: Cambridge University Press, 2006.

Kern, Stephanie. "Japan's Killer Quake." In *NOVA*, edited by Alan Ritsko, 60m. London, UK: PBS, 2011.

Kinnard, Douglas. *The War Managers*. Hanover, NH: University Press of New England, 1977.

Kozak, Warren. *Lemay: The Life and Wars of General Curtis Lemay*. New York, NY: Regenery Publishing, 2009.

Krepinevich, Andrew F. *The Army and Vietnam*. Baltimore, MD: Johns Hopkins University Press, 1986.

Lehrer, Jonah. *How We Decide*. Boston, MA: Houghton Mifflin Harcourt, 2009.

Manchester, William. *American Caesar*. Kindle ed. Boston, MA: Little, Brown and Co, 1978.

Marshall, S.L.A. *Notes on Urban Warfare*. Aberdeen Proving Ground, MD: U.S. Army Materiel Systems Analysis Agency, 1973.

Merriam-Webster Inc. *Merriam-Webster's Collegiate Dictionary*. Springfield, MA: Merriam-Webster, 2009.

Millett, Allan R. *The War for Korea, 1950-1951: They Came from the North*. Lawrence, KS: University Press of Kansas, 2010.

Morris, Ian, "Social Development", Stanford, CA http://www.ianmorris.org (course material accessed March 2012).

Mumford, Lewis. *The Culture of Cities*. New York, NY: Harcourt, 1938.

Mumford, Lewis. *The City in History: Its Origins, Its Transformations, and Its Prospects*. 1st ed. New York, NY: Harcourt, 1961.

Newman, David. *Boundaries, Territory and Postmodernity* Case Studies in Geopolitics. Portland, OR: F. Cass, 1999.

Noriega, Manuel. "Interview Concerning Just Cause." edited by Fernando Guadalupe. Fort Leavenworth, KS: School of Advanced Military Studies, 2007.

Norton, Richard J. "Feral Cities." *Naval War College Review* 56, no. 4 (2003).

Oberdorfer, Don. *Tet!* Baltimore, MD: Johns Hopkins University Press, 1971.

Operations Divison, U.S. Army Europe, "The U.S. Army in Berlin, 1945-1961," Heidelberg, GER.

Osinga, Frans P. B. *Science, Strategy and War: The Strategic Theory of John Boyd*. New York, NY: Routledge, 2007.

Payton, Robert J., "Lessons Learned for the Quarterly Period Ending 31 January 1968," San Francisco, CA.

Payton, Robert J., "Special Report of Observations, Reports, and Lessons Learned During Combat Conditions 31 January to 4 February 1968," San Francisco, CA.

Phillips, R. Cody, "Operation Just Cause: The Incursion into Panama," Washington, DC.

Plato and David Allan Bloom. *The Republic*. New York, NY: Basic Books, 1968.

Pohle, Victoria. *The Viet Cong in Saigon: Tactics and Objectives During the Tet Offensive* 1969. Vol. RM-5799-ISA/ARPA.

Programme United Nations Human Settlements. *State of the World's Cities 2010/2011: Bridging the Urban Divide*. Washington, DC: Earthscan, 2010.

Ralph, William W. "Improvised Destruction: Arnold, Lemay, and the Firebombing of Japan." *War in History* 13, no. 4 (2006): 495-522.

Rhodes, Richard. *Dark Sun: The Making of the Hydrogen Bomb*. New York, NY: Simon & Schuster, 2005.

Romjue, John L., "From Active Defense to Airland Battle: The Development of Army Doctrine 1973-1982," Fort Monroe, VA.

Rostker, Bernard. "The Evolution of the All-Volunteer Force." *Research Brief* (2006). [accessed 10 February 2013].

Rothbart, Daniel and K. V. Korostelina. *Why They Die: Civilian Devastation in Violent Conflict.* Ann Arbor, MI: University of Michigan Press, 2011.

Russ, Martin. *The Last Parallel.* New York, NY: Fromm International Publishing Corporation, 1957.

Said, Edward W. *Orientalism.* Vintage Books ed. New York, NY: Random House, 1994.

Schadlow, Nadia. "War and the Art of Governance." *Parameters: Journal of the US Army War College* 33, (2003): 85-94.

Senkovich, Steven W. "From Port Salines to Panama City: The Evolution of Command and Control in Contingency Operations." United States Army Command and General Staff College, 1991.

Sharp, Joanne P. *Geographies of Postcolonialism: Spaces of Power and Representation.* Los Angeles, CA: SAGE, 2009.

Shultz, Richard H. *In the Aftermath of War: United States' Support for Reconstruction and Nation-Building in Panama Following Just Cause.* Maxwell Air Force Base, AL: Airpower Research Institute, 1993.

Smith, Robert Ross. *Triumph in the Philippines* United States Army in World War II. The War in the Pacific. Washington, DC: Office of the Chief of Military History, Dept. of the Army, 1963.

Solnit, Rebecca. *Infinite City: A San Francisco Atlas.* Berkeley, CA: University of California Press, 2010.

Son, Pham Van, "The Viet Cong Tet Offensive (1968)," Saigon, Republic of Vietnam.

Sorely, Lewis. *Westmoreland: The General Who Lost Vietnam.* New York, NY: Houghton Mifflin Harcourt Publishing Company, 2011.

Spectorsky, Auguste C. *The Exurbanites.* New York, NY: Berkley Publishing Corp, 1955.

Staff, 6th USA, "Sixth United States Army Report on the Luzon Campaign 9 January 1945 - 30 June 1945," San Fransisco, CA.

Staff, XIV Corps, "After Action Report: XIV Corps M-1 Operation," Manila, Phillipines.

Stewart, Richard W. "The United States Army in Somalia, 1992-1994." edited by U.S. Army Center for Military History, 70-81-1. Fort Leavenworth, KS, 2002.

Summers, Harold. "The Strategic Perception of the Vietnam War." *Parameters* 13, no. 2 (1983): 11.

Swaykos, Joseph W. "Operational Art in the Tet Offensive: A North Vietnamese Perspective." Naval War College, 1996.

The Joint Staff. Joint Publication (JP) 3-06, *Joint Urban Operations*. Washington, DC: Headquarters, The Joint Staff, 2002.

The Joint Staff. Joint Publication (JP) 3-06, *Joint Urban Operations*. Washington, DC: Headquarters, The Joint Staff, 2009.

Turner, Charles A. P. "Did American Leadership Fail to Correctly Heed Indications of an Impending Offensive in the Months Preceding the Tet Offensive?" Command and General Staff College, 2003.

Tzu, Sun. *The Art of War*. Translated by Samuel B. Griffith. London, UK: Oxford Univ. Press, 1971.

Tzu, Sun. *The Art of War: The First English Translation Incorporating the Recently Discovered Yin-Ch'üeh-Shan Texts*. Translated by Roger T. Ames. New York, NY: Ballantine Books, 1993.

Tzu, Sun. *The Art of War*. Translated by Ralph D. Sawyer. Boulder, CO: Westview Press, 1994.

United Nations Human Settlements. *State of the World's Cities 2008/2009: Harmonious Cities*. Washington, DC: Earthscan, 2008.

United Nations Department of Economic and Social Affairs Population Division. "Population of Urban Agglomerations with 750,000 Inhabitants or More in 2011, by Country, 1950-2025 (Thousands)." In *Excel*, WUP2011-F12-Cities_Over_750K.xls. New York, NY: United Nations, 2011.

U.S. Agency for International Development Office of Military Affairs. *Stabilization and the District Stability Framework*. Washington, DC: U.S. Agency for International Development, 2010.

U.S. Army Peacekeeping and Stability Operations Institute. *Guiding Principles for Stablization and Reconstruction*. Carlisle, PA: United States Institute of Peace, 2009.

Washington, Robert F. Baumann and Lawrence A. Yates with Versalle F. *My Clan against the World* Military Case Studies, Edited by Lawyn C. Edwards. Fort Leavenworth, KS: Combat Studies Institute Press, 2003.

World Bank. *Reshaping Economic Geography* World Development Report. Washington, DC: World Bank, 2009.

World Bank. *World Development Report 2011: Conflict, Security, and Development* World Development Report. Washington, DC: The World Bank, 2011.

www.ingramcontent.com/pod-product-compliance
Lightning Source LLC
Chambersburg PA
CBHW080533290526
45790CB00006B/2389